Music Education

Music Education

Historical Contexts and Perspectives

Joseph A. Labuta

Wayne State University

Deborah A. Smith

Southern Illinois University-Edwardsville

 Prentice Hall, Upper Saddle River, New Jersey 07458

Library of Congress Cataloging-in-Publication Data

LABUTA, JOSEPH A.
    Music education : historical contexts and perspectives / Joseph A.
Labuta, Deborah A. Smith.
        p.   cm.
    Includes bibliographical references and index.
    ISBN   0–13–489444–8
    1. School music—Instruction and study—United States—History.
I. Smith, Deborah A., (date).   II. Title.
MT3.U5L23   1997
780′.71′073—dc20   96-24983
                                                    CIP
                                                    MN

Editorial director: *Charlyce Jones Owen*
Acquisitions editor: *Bud Therien*
Editorial/production supervision: *Kim Gueterman*
Marketing manager: *Alison Pendergast*
Cover director and designer: *Jayne Conte*
Buyer: *Bob Anderson*

This book was set in 10/12 Times Roman by TCSystems, Inc.
and was printed and bound by R.R. Donnelley & Sons Company.
The cover was printed by The Lehigh Press, Inc.

   © 1997 by Prentice-Hall, Inc.
Simon & Schuster/A Viacom Company
Upper Saddle River, New Jersey   07458

Printed in the United States of America
10   9   8   7   6   5   4   3   2

ISBN   0-13-489444-8

Prentice-Hall International (UK) Limited, *London*
Prentice-Hall of Australia Pty. Limited, *Sydney*
Prentice-Hall of Canada Inc., *Toronto*
Prentice-Hall Hispanoamericana, S.A., *Mexico*
Prentice-Hall of India Private Limited, *New Delhi*
Prentice-Hall of Japan, Inc., *Tokyo*
Simon & Schuster Asia Pte. Ltd., *Singapore*
Editora Prentice-Hall do Brasil, Ltda., *Rio de Janeiro*

Contents

Preface

This examination of music education is based on two premises: (1) The status of music education in any society reflects general philosophical viewpoints about the nature of music, its purpose, and its value; and (2) music education history reveals recurring themes or cycles on which shrewd guesses about the discipline's future can be based. Thus, philosophy and history are unifying elements of this presentation, which provides a conceptual foundation for further study.

The text is divided into three major sections. Part I, "Music Education: A Reflection of Philosophy," establishes groundwork for the remainder of the presentation. The first chapter, "A History of Public School Music in America," touches on people, places, events, and ideas as it explores the history of music in American schools from the colonial period through 1980. Because music education is part of broader societal and educational systems, general or nonmusical events influencing its development are also examined. "Philosophies of Music Education," the second chapter in Part I, examines information from the first chapter in light of music and education philosophies to clarify relationships between these and events in music education history. The chapter concludes with a working philosophy of American music education.

Part II, "Music Education: Philosophy in Action," includes chapters 3 through 5. Chapter 3, "Curriculum: A Model for Music Instruction," discusses philosophical and historical influences on the content and development of music curricula. "Music Learning," the fourth chapter, presents a general definition of learning and an explanation of how music learning occurs. Chapter 5, "Music Teaching," focuses on relationships among philosophy, instruction, and learning. Teacher responsibilities and their effects on learning are examined to clarify the philosophical bases of selected teaching methods that American music educators use.

The last part of the text, "Music Education: Toward the Future," includes Chapter 6, "America Education since 1980," and Chapter 7, "Where Does Music Education Go from Here?" Chapter 6 examines trends in education since 1980. Chapter 7 looks for ways in which all of the preceding information suggests music education's future direction, evoking ideas rather than providing answers; the reader participates in speculating about the profession's future.

To provide a holistic perspective of music education while examining its various facets, each section begins with a general introduction suggesting relationships between previously presented information and the material to be covered and establishing content objectives. For the same reason, each chapter concludes with questions that require synthesizing and applying information.

Because this text aims to increase understanding of the current state of music in U.S. schools by providing information about its development, the only prerequisite for reading it is an interest in school music. An important objective of the text, however, particularly for readers who are also music educators, is to encourage critical thinking and foresight, which are so important for professional and societal growth.

The perspective presented here is one of many. The authors merely offer a starting point for discussion, investigation, and analysis. Moreover, they encourage dialogue—between themselves and the reader and, in class settings, among the readers themselves. Discussions juxtaposing various perspectives stimulate clarity and growth for everyone involved.

Music Education

Part I

Music Education: A Reflection of Philosophy

The transmission of history, values, culture, ideas, vocational skills, and religious beliefs from one group of people to another both sustains and is a natural consequence of any continuous interaction among people in groups, that is, of communal life. All societal units— families, friends and neighbors, religious organizations or churches, professional groups and political parties—share responsibility for passing information to members of the larger community, and the process by which this transmission occurs is generally called education.

In ancient and prehistoric societies informal, primarily oral rote education was sufficient. But in more modern societies, in which knowledge and skills increased constantly and rapidly, this transmission could no longer be left to chance. Institutions or schools were established to facilitate the process. The primary purpose of all schooling[1] is communal: It promotes individual development for the benefit of society. This communal nature of schooling persists from one generation to another even when changing societal needs require that instructional methods and curriculum content be modified. Yet because societies throughout modern history have recognized the crucial role schooling plays in societal well-being, virtually every aspect of communal life has, at one time or another, been nominated for inclusion in school curricula.

why?   Discussions of whether music should be transmitted in schools have gone on for centuries. Even among those who agree that music merits a permanent place in schooling, there are debates about how it should be taught, why, and by whom. One reason for this lack of consensus is that music only contributes to education fully when students study it *as* music. Unlike subjects such as reading and mathematics, whose general objectives do not depend on whether they function as means or ends, music's contribution to general education diminishes if its overt, non-artistic outcomes (i.e., discipline, higher levels of

---

[1] As used in this text, *schooling* denotes an institutionalized transmission process intended to convey information in a systematic, organized, and sequential manner.

1

achievement and self-esteem, motivation) supersede its covert, artistic ones (i.e., increased sensitivity to and appreciation for beauty, a desire for quality). Whenever this happens, music becomes like other school subjects except that they can achieve the same nonartistic outcomes for less time and money.

Aside from minimizing music's unique contribution to education, a nonartistic or nonmusical approach to school music creates a void that is difficult to fill. Apart from other fine arts disciplines, no school subject provides as much insight into quality of life than music. Thus, school music must indeed be musical and use musical processes to achieve musical outcomes if it is to realize its potential in general education. At the same time, it must contribute to achieving general educational goals established by society. This dual identity accounts for many problematic aspects of music instruction in schools.

In some ways, music education's identity and potential contribution to schooling are less clear now than in the past, but examining ways in which past societies and educators viewed school music is instructive.

The primary objective of Part I is to explore the history of music education in American schools and the philosophical bases underlying its development. The development of philosophies of music in Western civilization is also important here, and much of the discussion in Chapter 2 focuses on the philosophical contexts in which music education has evolved.

1

A History
of Public School Music
in America

INTRODUCTION AND OBJECTIVES

When, how, and why did music become a part of American public education? This chapter presents a comprehensive history of music education in America from the colonial period through 1980. The reasons for studying events of ten or twenty years ago may be fairly clear, but what possible relationship could exist between something that happened over 200 years ago and events that occurred a decade ago?

To begin with, the quality and status of what exists now are often determined by what existed in the past. Things become or do not become, people develop or do not develop, situations improve or do not improve. Past events create a standard by which change is measured and evaluated. *Is this true?*

In addition, past events are the roots of current ones, and current events influence the future. Things do not happen in a vacuum, out of the blue. To be interpreted accurately, events must be examined in light of the circumstances preceding them. Prospective employers ask for résumés and doctors ask for medical histories for the same reason: Events in an employee's or patient's past help the employer or doctor to understand who the person is now and, to some degree, who the person will be one, three, or five years from now.

This chapter uses a contextualist approach to provide general knowledge about events that shaped public school music education in the United States. A *contextualist approach* to history is characterized by "an immersion in the detailed circumstances of a distant era and an effort to understand that world not as it anticipated the future but as it was experienced by those who lived it."[1] Ideologies generating these events are also discussed so that relationships between "then" and "now" become more apparent.

---

[1] Bernard Bailyn, *The Ideological Origins of the American Revolution,* enlarged ed. (Cambridge, MA: Belknap Press, 1992), v.

After completing Chapter 1, readers should be able to do the following for each major period identified in American music education history:

- Describe the organization or structure of general education and music education.
- Discuss social and philosophical influences on general education and music education.
- Name important individuals in general and music education; describe their contributions and achievements, and, where appropriate, describe the nature of their influence.
- Compare the approaches to general and music education in any two major historical periods.
- Identify important social, philosophical, and educational events or publications and describe their influence.

THE COLONIAL AND REVOLUTIONARY WAR PERIODS (1600–1800)

The Seventeenth Century

Several groups settled along the eastern coast of the New World during the seventeenth century.[2] Each group's ethnicity, religious orientation, and reasons for immigration shaped the communities they established and helped to account for variations among early American colonies.

The first settlers arrived in Virginia in 1607 to establish a colony for King James of England and to save Native Americans from heathenism and Catholicism by converting them to Anglicanism. Twelve years later, a small group of African immigrants joined this Jamestown colony, arriving on a Dutch ship. According to some historians, these twenty Africans were indentured servants, like numerous white colonists: after a period of servitude, they would be freemen. Others maintain that they were slaves rather than servants and were thus treated differently from their first days in the colony. In any case, black colonists were soon enslaved, with no voice in colonial policies. By 1650, both Virginia and Maryland (established in 1634) relied heavily on slave labor.

In 1624, Dutch Calvinists arrived in the New World and established settlements in New Netherland (along the Hudson and lower Delaware rivers), where immigrants from Finland, Sweden, Portugal, France, Belgium, and England would settle later. Over the next thirty-eight years, this area became the most ethnically and religiously diverse of the colonies, with laws and public announcements printed or read publicly in Dutch, German, and English.[3]

The New World offered religious freedom without the loss of English citizenship for Separatists, whose dissatisfaction with the Church of England had motivated them to dis-

---

[2] See Lawrence A. Cremin, *American Education: The Colonial Experience, 1607–1783* (New York: Harper and Row, 1970), 3–30.

[3] Ibid., 18–20.

sociate from it and form their own congregations. These lower- and middle-class Pilgrims established colonies in what is now Massachusetts, approximately 600 miles north of Jamestown. They named their settlement Plymouth, after the English city where they had traded their first ship, *Speedwell,* for the more seaworthy *Mayflower.*

Puritans were also northern settlers who, like the Separatists, were displeased with the Anglican Church, but the Puritans attempted to reform it rather than separate. Led by John Winthrop, these landowners and clergy set sail for America in March 1630. They reached Cape Ann, near Salem, Massachusetts, in June, found it unsatisfactory, and decided to establish a temporary settlement on the Charlestown peninsula. Later, amid disease and rumors of attacks by the French, members of Winthrop's group dispersed, settling in seven adjacent towns, one of which became Boston.

Winthrop's ideology guided daily life in and around Boston.[4] He envisioned a centralized and thoroughly religious community devoid of the individualism, avarice, and human suffering that he saw generated by English commerce. He believed that societal divisions were ordained by God and that God's plan was for the wealthy to rule society in the interest of the people. In Winthrop's ideal society, personal gain would be valued only if it benefitted the community. Beyond this, the people's covenant with God—to be the people of God and to be governed by God's will—would ensure that they adhered to this plan and their places in it.

General Education Practices

Colonial education followed European models, emphasizing religious and civic instruction and restricted to males. In addition, though not explicitly limited to particular social classes, educational approaches were usually determined by socioeconomic factors. In the South, for instance, private tutors provided in-home instruction for children of affluent families, but the only academic education most southern children received was derived from catechism, worship services, and *apprenticeships* that met the South's immediate economic or political goals. Boys between ages ten and fourteen (and, on occasion, girls as young as age five) were apprenticed, or "put out," to learn a manual trade or "calling" that would make them independent, self-supporting, contributing members of society. During the apprenticeship, which lasted approximately seven years, all aspects of these children's welfare were the responsibility of the adults with whom they lived. Because the intended outcome of this educational approach was to develop skilled laborers rather than societal leaders, these children received minimal academic instruction. They learned only enough reading and writing to understand the Bible and public ordinances and to ply their craft.[5]

The middle colonies' interest in education was greater than in the South. Cultural and religious groups intent on maintaining their identity developed a variety of educational systems. Education was most valued in northern communities, however, because Puritans

---

[4] See Darrett B. Rutman, *Winthrop's Boston* (Chapel Hill: University of North Carolina Press, 1965).

[5] See Cremin, *American Education: The Colonial Experience,* 120–122, 133–134; and Joel Spring, *The American School: 1642–1990,* 2d ed. (New York: Longman, 1990), 5–13.

believed eternal salvation depended on it. Their education system aimed to shape depraved human consciences in accordance with their religious tenets. It is not surprising, then, that all families in Massachusetts were required to educate their children in reading, religious principles, and colony laws. In addition, towns of fifty householders were required by law to appoint reading and writing teachers; those with 100 or more householders had to establish grammar schools.

Though apprenticeships were common in all of the colonies, *reading and writing schools* were most likely to be found in middle and northern areas. Home schools provided practical, rudimentary knowledge in reading, writing, and ciphering. Instruction was primarily oral, taught on an each-one-teach-one basis by parents, other adults, siblings, or peers. For children from homes in which no one was able to provide instruction, servants, tutors, or neighborhood housewives held reading classes in their homes. In these *petty* or *dame schools* children learned to read from hornbooks or ABCs, primers, catechisms, the Bible, or one of the devotional publications popular during this period.[6]

Grammar schools, found mainly in the North, offered the most distinctive approach to education in early America. Like their European models, these schools were held outside of the household and provided the most formal and systematic schooling available. Because they prepared children for advanced study and leadership roles in society, the grammar schools' comprehensive liberal arts curriculum was determined by the content of European college entrance examinations and included English grammar, Latin, Greek, and Hebrew.[7]

Music in the Early Colonies

There was no systematic music instruction in the South, although some colonists played instruments and were musically literate. Southern children and adults learned to sing and read music by participating in religious services. Lutherans, Quakers, Catholics, Calvinists, Anglicans, Anabaptists, Jews, and other religious groups in the middle colonies also included some type of music in their worship services. As in the South, incidental and rote learning were largely responsible for perpetuating musical traditions in these colonies.[8]

In contrast, the Pilgrims' musical tradition, instilled in them by their founder, Robert Browne, was a vital part of their worship. For this reason, the *Book of Psalmes: Englished Both in Prose and Metre* (published in 1612 and also called the *Ainsworth Psalter* after its compiler, Henry Ainsworth) was among the valued possessions they brought to Massachusetts. The simplest of this Psalter's thirty-nine psalm tunes were used more frequently,

---

[6] See Cremin, *American Education: The Colonial Experience,* 128–134; and Spring, *The American School: 1642–1990,* 5–13.

[7] Cremin, *American Education: The Colonial Experience,* 181–187.

[8] Michael L. Mark and Charles L. Gary, *A History of American Music Education* (New York: Schirmer Books, 1992), 44–58; and James A. Keene, *A History of Music Education in the United States* (Hanover, NH: University Press of New England, 1982), 1–12.

and as time passed, complex tunes were forgotten. By late in the century, only about twelve melodies were well-known and used regularly.[9]

Similarly, although the Psalter that the Puritans brought to America, called the *Whole Book of Psalms* (or the *Sternhold and Hopkins Psalter,* 1562), contained sixty-five folklike melodies, congregations favored the easiest melodies as memories of more complex ones faded. *The Bay Psalm Book (The Whole Booke of Psalmes Faithfully Translated into English Metre),* published in 1640, reflected this tendency in that its six metrical schemes used shorter, easier melodies.

The *Bay Psalm Book* became extremely popular not only in Boston and Plymouth but in Europe. Of its numerous editions, the ninth (1698) is particularly noteworthy. In addition to being the first to include music notation (treble and bass parts for thirteen psalm tunes), this revision promoted two informal types of music learning that were gaining popularity in the colonies toward the end of the seventeenth century: (1) letters for *fasola* solmization using the four-note gamut (mi, fa, so, and la), and (2) instructions for performing psalms correctly and reading music. These additions allowed colonists to learn the rudiments of psalm singing on their own.[10]

Although much of the musical activity in these settlements stemmed from religious activities, colonists owned virginals, lutes, citterns, viols and violins, and woodwind instruments and apparently both secular (recreational) and instrumental music, although differing regionally, were alive and well in early America. In the South in particular, "parlor music" became a desirable, even expected, aspect of quasi-aristocratic life, and much leisure time was devoted to informal music making. But whereas southern and middle-colony attitudes toward secular music were somewhat relaxed, the North's austere psalm-singing tradition and its restrictions on secular musical activity have been taken as indications that northerners (particularly Puritans) actually disliked music. On the contrary, their attitudes toward music were moralistic rather than antagonistic or intolerant. Northern leaders attempted to control instrumental and secular music because these were closely associated with worldliness, but they advocated and encouraged recreational psalm singing.

By the end of the seventeenth century, the colonial population had more than quadrupled. Colonization was under way in Arkansas and the Carolinas. Two discontented ministers from the Massachusetts Bay colony—Thomas Hooker and Roger Williams—had established thriving colonies in Connecticut and Rhode Island, respectively, while northern New England was also developing. The mid-Atlantic settlements of Pennsylvania (which included part of what is now Delaware and New Jersey) were rivaling New Netherland as the most ethnically and religiously diverse. Of these three colonial groups, the South remained under the most ironbound British control. European control over the middle colonies, although not as strong as in the South, remained fairly secure, but Massachusetts reestablished its independence from the crown in 1688.

It was also apparent that the growing system of black slavery would eventually have far-reaching consequences for the young nation, although many colonists refused to have

---

[9] Ibid.

[10] Mark and Gary, *A History of American Music Education,* 62–65; and Keene, *A History of Music Education in the United States,* 1–12.

slaves. Quakers in eastern Pennsylvania promoted ideas that would eventually lead to the abolitionist movement. Thus, the demands of agriculture notwithstanding, "many in the Middle Colonies welcomed the arguments against slavery that became more pronounced during the Revolutionary Period."[11]

The Eighteenth Century

During the late seventeenth and well into the eighteenth century, Sir Isaac Newton (1643–1727) and, to a greater extent, John Locke (1632–1704) inspired a new view of the world that stimulated and revolutionized thinking while generating controversy and far-reaching changes that would eventually affect every aspect of American life. Newton stressed human intelligence and rationalism. Rather than portraying the universe as a mysterious creation, he focused on its knowability. For him, the world was part of a cosmos whose workings were revealed by God through nature. Locke applauded Newton's rationalism, but also believed that experience and experiment were equally valid ways of knowing the universe.

These men's ideas created the intellectual and social context for revolution on both sides of the Atlantic, although the effects were perhaps more pronounced in the New World.[12] For most colonists, settling in America had been the first step toward fulfilling humanity's promise and rectifying errors and injustices of past generations. They believed that the New World *had* to be different, although its destiny and the manner in which it would be achieved were far from settled. After Newton and Locke, however, the means and ends became clearer as a uniquely American perspective crystallized.

Newton's orderliness and rationalism and Locke's emphasis on the value of experience in humankind's search for understanding evoked pronounced differences of opinion as Europeans and Americans sought to translate new theories about nature, reason, and experience into modes of action that would meet the needs of changing societies. The upheaval was widespread. Religious differences, for example, had always been a part of colonial life, but the Enlightenment caused internal fragmentation. Most denominations divided into Old Light (traditional) and New Light (enlightened) camps while other colonists moved toward a religion that was more rational and philosophical than theological. Prominent among these deists were Benjamin Franklin (1706–1790), Thomas Jefferson (1743–1826), Ethan Allen (1738–1789), and Thomas Paine (1737–1809).[13]

Because religious groups disagreed about the value of learning and knowledge, they also disagreed about educational objectives and methods. Generally, deists and Old Lights supported classical education, whereas New Lights decried it, stressing conversion experiences instead. Similarly, there were opposing views about the relative merits of "useful"

---

[11] John Hope Franklin, *From Slavery to Freedom: A History of Negro Americans,* 5th ed. (New York: Alfred A. Knopf, Inc., 1980), 62–63.

[12] For an in-depth discussion of this ideological development, see Bernard Bailyn, *The Ideological Origins of the American Revolution,* enlarged ed. (Cambridge, MA: Belknap Press, 1992); and Peter Gay, *The Enlightenment: An Interpretation—The Science of Freedom* (New York: W. W. Norton and Company, 1969).

[13] See Henry F. May, *The Enlightenment in America* (Oxford: Oxford University Press, 1976); and Cremin, *American Education: The Colonial Experience,* 310–336.

and "ornamental" education—schooling that earned or confirmed status, respectively—in a free and economically healthy society.

As controversy mounted, the need for societal balance became urgent; America could not fulfill its destiny as long as its people remained divided. Compromise became America's watchword. Over time many colonists adopted a middle-of-the-road religious philosophy that offended no one and had wide appeal. Meanwhile, educational institutions gradually adopted a curriculum designed to develop ethics and morals without endorsing a specific religious creed.

General Education Practices

Some changes in American schooling foreshadowed trends that became more pronounced during the next century. Whereas shaping pious and virtuous individuals had been the foremost educational goal in the seventeenth century, schooling in the eighteenth century focused on meeting immediate societal goals and began to respond to the concerns, needs, and values of specific ethnic and cultural groups. Philadelphia, for instance, had become an educational and cultural center that attracted many immigrants, which caused Franklin and other Philadelphians concern that the city's predominantly English culture would be overtaken by other cultures, particularly Germanic. To prevent this, they organized free English-language schools for immigrant children. Anglicization was the primary purpose of these *charity schools.*[14]

Schools for children of free black citizens were also organized during this period. Some black manumissioned adults in the North and Midwest who were concerned about their children's education could afford to send them to private schools, but many more could not. Yet because of the hostility black children often experienced in free schools, few of them attended those institutions. By 1792 Philadelphia, New York, Boston, and Baltimore had opened segregated schools. Quakers were especially active in promoting early efforts to educate the children of freed northern slaves.[15]

As national expansion pushed the country westward, land ordinances dating from this time officially endorsed education. In particular, the Northwest Ordinance of 1787 mandated that, rather than being given away, a central mile-square plot in each new region be rented and that revenue generated by these rentals be used to establish schools and defray general educational expenses. This Congressional support of education signaled movement toward publically funded schools—an objective realized later in *common schools.*

Another change in the country's educational structure was the dramatic increase in academies and colleges. These institutions blossomed as popular concern about freedom of thought and the importance of "useful" knowledge led to reaction against the classical liberal arts curriculum offered by existing institutions of higher learning. Whereas only

---

[14] See Cremin, *American Education: The Colonial Experience,* 256–264; Spring, 13–17; and Carl F. Kaestle, *Pillars of the Republic: Common Schools and American Society, 1780–1860* (New York: Hill and Wang, 1983), 30–61.

[15] See Kaestle, *Pillars of the Republic,* 30–61.

nine had been established prior to the Revolutionary War, approximately 250 colleges and academies opened between that war and the Civil War. Expansion of higher education gained additional impetus from the Morril Land Grant Act of 1862, which allocated land to each state for establishing colleges to aid agriculture and industry.

Music in Eighteenth-Century America

At the beginning of the eighteenth century, many northerners were distressed by the state of music in worship.[16] Poor musical skills, the lack of systematic music instruction, fading memories, and ordinances against instrumental accompaniments had contributed to its erosion in spite of *fasola,* simplified melodies, and self-instruction tools. Moreover, the high illiteracy rate among worshippers (which now included slaves and unschooled laborers) restricted the use of printed material.

When similar deterioration had occurred in England, church leaders recommended that psalm tunes be "lined out" (a process also known as deaconing) so that all congregants could participate in the singing. The deacon or song leader "tuned the psalm" by chanting one or two lines of the psalm text alone (on the first or fifth note of the scale, depending on the melody) before the congregation sang the lines. The deacon's primary task was to give text; the psalm tune or melody was not usually given. Thus, lining out required that congregants have prior knowledge of psalm tunes. Lining out or deaconing was used in some colonies by the mid 1600s, and most churches in New England had adopted it by 1700. The practice would have worked well except that song leaders tended to speak rather than sing the text. In addition, those who *did* sing often added ornaments, and some congregants improvised or embellished the melody when they echoed it. The congregational singing that resulted was anything but uniform and harmonious, but worshippers resisted acquiring music reading skills. The unregulated, spontaneous singing style that reformers perceived as "deplorably uncouth" was for others a treasured tradition.

Even so, reformers exerted considerable pressure. John Tufts' *An Introduction to the Singing of Psalm-Tunes* (1721) encouraged singing by note as the only acceptable way of praising God. To simplify music reading, he replaced note heads with the first letter of each syllable in the four-note gamut (mi, fa, so, la) and used various punctuation marks after notes to indicate their duration. Music in his book was followed by practical information about music and singing.

Tufts' book was the first colonial psalmbook to contain English music exclusively. In addition, his synthesis of practices gained acceptance in colonial church music, and his attempt to simplify music reading for nonmusicians and to teach women and children how to sing were noteworthy. Another self-instruction psalmbook, *The Grounds and Rules of Musick Explained (An Introduction to the Art of Singing by Note),* by the Reverend Thomas Walter, also became available in 1721. This publication included three-part harmonizations of psalms in traditional notation and may have been intended for people who already possessed some musical knowledge.[17]

---

[16] See Mark and Gary, 65–81; and Keene, 1–12.

[17] See Keene, 13–28; and Mark and Gary, 65–70.

The high quality of music performed by some religious groups in the middle colonies inspired others to improve the music in their services. Especially influential were the German Moravians, who brought a rich musical tradition to Pennsylvania. This religious sect emphasized music instruction and public performances of choral and brass instrumental music. The religious community at Ephrata in what is now Lancaster County, Pennsylvania, also elevated the quality of religious music in the middle and northern colonies.[18] Georg Konrad Beisel (1691–1768), the commune's leader and founder, and his Solitarys (so called because of their solitary lifestyle) established their permanent site in 1732. Some of the earliest collections of original America music emerged from this community, later called the Ephrata Cloisters, which was well known for its beautiful musical performances. A number of factors—Moravian musical excellence, the achievements of Biesel's commune, the decline of church music performance in the northern colonies, and resistance to various reform efforts—defined the musical context in which *singing schools* developed and flourished as the first formal attempt to improve music reading and singing skills.

Two types of singing schools developed in New England during the early 1700s.[19] *Congregational schools,* sponsored by specific churches for their members, held classes in rented rooms or singers' homes. Students supplied their own tune books and paid one dollar for three months of instruction, with the remainder of the instructor's wages and the cost of additional instructional materials paid from church funds. *Independently sponsored schools* also lasted approximately three months but were organized by the instructor, who announced the beginning of classes in local newspapers and newsletters. Nondenominational classes met two or three days each week in empty rooms at taverns, in local schoolhouses or town halls, or in citizens' homes.

Some singing-school masters were immigrants or former singing-school students, although most were native-born, self-taught musicians. Few made their living solely from teaching music. Some maintained a residence and worked regularly at a trade, but most were itinerants who frequently taught at more than one school. The majority of singing-school masters composed the music in the tune books used in their schools.[20]

Singing-school courses usually culminated in a public performance, and colonists who attended these schools also sang for funerals, dedications, ordinations, and other public assemblies. Over time choirs formed as more skilled singers in congregations began sitting together in special sections of their churches. Like most deviations from tradition, these new choirs created considerable dissention among congregants through the end of the century.[21]

Secular music became more prominent in eighteenth-century colonial life, particularly in the South and in port towns, where the growing "middling" class of plantation owners, shipbuilders, and merchants sought to acquire all the trappings of English aristocracy and elegant living. As these colonial "gentle folk" attained the socioeconomic sta-

[18] See Everette Gordon Alderfer, *The Ephrata Commune: An Early American Counterculture* (Pittsburgh: University of Pittsburgh Press, 1985).

[19] See Kenneth Silverman, *A Cultural History of the American Revolution* (New York: Columbia University Press, 1987), 191–195.

[20] Ibid.

[21] Ibid.

tus that afforded "leisure to cultivate the finer arts and improve the common stock of knowledge,"[22] they also became amateur musicians.

These musicians purchased small locally made instruments from immigrant music makers and ordered larger instruments directly from London or from colonial music dealers who maintained a stock of imported instruments. English theater music was also available to them through imported magazines and local publications that could be purchased from booksellers and printers, who also received regular shipments of works by Handel, Vivaldi, Corelli, and other European composers.[23]

Women studied voice and guitar, men received instruction on violin and flute (which was especially popular in the colonies), and the harpsichord and spinet were popular with both sexes. Their teachers were itinerant "professors of music," most of whom had been trained in Europe and offered group or private instruction for a fee. Like their singing-school counterparts, these instructors survived by being versatile: They were performers, music copyists, or instructors of various nonmusical disciplines (including the social graces) as their situations demanded.

Slaves also contributed substantially to musical activity in the colonies, particularly on southern plantations, where they frequently supplied the music for dances, informal concerts, and general plantation merriment. Although the majority of these self-taught musicians were fiddlers, many others played the French horn, fife, or drums. Some who did not play instruments became known for their singing, whistling, or instrument making. Frequently, slave musicians were local celebrities to some extent, although their musical abilities also benefitted slave owners: Such skills increased a slave's market value and were used to identify and capture runaways.

Larger cities of the prerevolutionary period offered public concerts, but with the exception of the singing schools, musical activities in urban areas dwindled considerably during the American Revolution. However, instrumental music performance was the most prevalent activity in army camps and on battlefields. Many fife and drum corps and military bands organized during this period received governmental support and often presented concerts, usually in rural areas. When peace returned, musical life in the colonies resumed with increased vigor. Musician-veterans and immigrant musicians offered larger and more frequent concerts as a new wave of songbook publishing began, following publication of the Reverend James Lyon's *Urania* (1761), which contained instructions about music and singing along with previously unavailable American and English compositions. This new music introduced colonists to ornamentation, dotted rhythms, and text painting, but Lyon's inclusion of seventy English "fuguing psalm tunes" was of greatest importance for the development of American music.[24]

Whereas hymns and anthems had appeared in the colonies approximately thirty years earlier, fuguing tunes were entirely new to Americans and sparked considerable interest among singers while capturing the imagination of singing-school masters and com-

[22] Benjamin Franklin, *The Autobiography and Other Writings,* selected and edited by L. Jesse Lemisch (New York: New American Library, 1961), 206.

[23] See Kenneth Silverman, *A Cultural History of the American Revolution.*

[24] Ibid., 45–46.

posers. Numerous new songbooks were published, and the number of American compositions they included was greater than ever before. (Only about twelve of the hundreds of
musical compositions published in the colonies prior to this time had been written by native-born citizens.) One American composer who gained recognition during this period
was William Billings (1746–1800), a self-taught musician from Boston and a tanner by
trade. Billings's first song collection, *The New England Psalm Singer,* or *American Cho-
rister* (1770), contained more than 100 of his own compositions.[25]

While Billings's a cappella, ornamented, and imitative folk style was gaining popularity in the colonies, Europe moved toward the homophonic and relatively plain Classical style. This, along with the increasing secularization of American music and the singing
school's emphasis on technical proficiency, led to disagreements about musical style, evident in the rivalry between William Billings and his American-born contemporary, An-
drew Law (1749–1821). Billings's music was more virtuosic than devotional or worship-
ful. He preferred the raucous ornamented singing of powerful and energetic musical
compositions to the soft, refined, somber style of Law and similar composers.

Cultivated taste gradually shifted to homophonic compositions with unadorned so-
prano melodies, so that by the end of the eighteenth century "good taste" in colonial choral
music was exemplified by the "scientific" chordal European style. Major tonalities, common time, and slower tempi prevailed, as a new reform of American church music revived
old psalm tunes in harmonized, chordal textures. Also by the turn of the century, northern
singing-school masters took their expertise to the South, where music education thrived
and public demand for more sophisticated musical performances increased.

Instrumental music instruction also became more prevalent. The piano replaced the
spinet and harpsichord as the most popular household instrument, and organ music rivaled
choirs for primacy in churches. Community musical and choral societies flourished
throughout the colonies to provide new challenges and performance opportunities for
those skilled in reading music. Similarly, universities and academies established societies
for music study and performance. Many of these became part of the curriculum.

Music performance also appeared to help solve an urgent societal dilemma. Postwar
leaders believed that group singing was an ideal way to develop cooperative spirit and prepare youngsters to assume democratic responsibilities. According to Dr. Benjamin Rush
(1746–1813), for instance, "Mechanical effects in civilizing the mind, and thereby preparing it for the influence of religion and government, have been so often felt and recorded,
that it will be unnecessary to mention facts in favour of its usefulness."[26]

THE NATIONAL PERIOD (1800–1880)

Overall, America's population rose approximately 35 percent per decade from 1830 to
1860. As economic and industrial growth pushed American society from agriculture toward industrialization, the proportion of Americans living in urban areas grew, with

[25] Ibid., 198–209.
[26] Ibid., 477.

Philadelphia, Boston, New York, and Baltimore showing population increases of as much as 156 percent. Immigration continued unabated, and American-born families and single young adults migrated to northern port towns, where chances for employment seemed greatest. At the same time rural population also increased, as many other people settled in the West.[27]

Crime, drunkenness, and other types of undesirable behavior plaqued the crowded cities. Some organizations previously concerned with wisdom, religion, or philosophy shifted their efforts to ameliorating social problems. Similarly, educational institutions slowly assumed the family's role in educating and socializing children. Juvenile reformatories (called "houses of refuge") and additional charity schools were established to provide the nation's poor and immigrant families with a child-rearing environment that was free of criminal elements and would help develop sound moral character.[28]

Even so, in the wake of the Revolutionary War, national leaders became increasingly concerned about securing America's independence and progress. They believed the nation's survival required balancing freedom and order, instilling patriotism, and educating Americans about their new Constitution. They saw as crucial the development of individuals who were intellectually, morally, and culturally equipped to assume leadership responsibilities without being corrupted by such authority. Concluding that schooling could meet these national needs if it provided an equal moral, civic, and academic education for every American citizen, this new group of leaders set about engineering an educational system that would produce a perfect society.

The Common School Movement

Common schools, as conceived by their developers and promoters, may be described as "[schools] under state control teaching a common body of knowledge to students from different backgrounds" or "[schools] that were attended in common by all children and in which a common political and social ideology was taught,"[29] but neither of these descriptions adequately conveys the extent to which these institutions were meant to be "common." Reformers actually envisioned schooling devoid of ethnic, moral, economic, religious, political, social, curricular, and regional differences.

Horace Mann (1796–1859), the "father of the common school," was born into a Calvinist family of farmers in Franklin, Massachusetts. After completing law studies at Brown University and passing the bar examination, he began practicing law. From 1823 through 1837, Mann was a member of the Massachusetts legislature and was instrumental in passing laws regulating the lottery and limiting the sale of alcohol. He helped organize the state's Board of Education, worked to improve conditions in prisons and insane asy-

---

[27] Kaestle, 13–61. Also see Charles Sellers, *The Market Revolution: Jacksonian America, 1815–1846* (New York: Oxford Press, 1990).

[28] Spring, 53–59; 78–92.

[29] Spring, *The American School,* 74. For additional information about common schools, see Lawrence A. Cremin, *American Education: The National Experience, 1783–1876* (New York: Harper and Row, 1980), 133–175: Spring, 70–92; and David Tyack and Elisabeth Hansot, *Managers of Virtue: Public School Leadership in America, 1820–1980* (New York: Basic Books, 1982), 28–71.

lums, and was eventually elected president of the state senate. Yet he remained deeply troubled about what he perceived to be the deterioration of American society.

By 1837, when Mann was asked to serve as secretary for the Massachusetts Board of Education, he was convinced that schooling was the key to regenerating society but that the existing educational structure was inadequate. Local control of schooling made it impossible to ensure proper instruction, particularly because educational decisions were often made by people who were inadequately educated themselves. Moreover, far too many teachers were ill-prepared to convey the knowledge or fit the role model that young Americans needed. Furthermore, numerous children rarely or never attended school; the cost of education made it inaccessible, especially for large lower-income families. Mann promoted schools that were "free, financed by local and state government, controlled by lay boards of education, mixing all social groups under one roof, and offering education of such quality that no parent would desire private schooling."[30] In these institutions, all of America's children would receive common, nonsectarian moral instruction; would be imbued with a common, nonpartisan political creed; and would ultimately share a common social class. Education would be "the great equalizer of the conditions of men—the balance-wheel of the social machinery."[31]

Although Mann is the person most often associated with the ideology and eventual implementation of public education, hundreds supported the cause and worked tirelessly to ensure its success. A significant number of these were women. Catharine E. Beecher (1800–1878), Mary Lyon (1797–1849), and Emma Hart Willard (1787–1870) expanded educational opportunities for females and elevated women's social status by promoting free public education. They argued that the female's role in shaping the character of republican citizens was ordained by God and required that they be actively involved in schools as teachers. Furthermore, these women maintained that instead of being a replacement for motherhood as many men feared, teaching was the perfect preparation for it.

This concept of "republican motherhood" addressed one of the deepest concerns of common school advocates: establishing a nurturing, stable, and inexpensive teaching force. Developing sound character and instilling a strong sense of morals and ethics in the new republic's young people required teachers who were themselves of strong character and high morals. Given the lifestyle of many male teachers, most people agreed that women were better suited for this role. But beyond these qualities, teachers had to be academically prepared and trained in teaching. Willard opened a boarding school for girls in her home in 1814 and founded the Troy Female Seminary in 1821 for the purpose of educating women to be responsible mothers and teachers. In 1837, Lyon opened Mount Holyoke Seminary for Women. Similarly, Beecher, who believed that teaching was a distinctly feminine vocation, actively recruited women for teacher training and established the Western Female Institute of Cincinnati.[32]

[30] David Tyack and Elizabeth Hansot, *Managers of Virtue: Public School Leadership in America, 1820–1982* (New York: Basic Books, 1982), 30.

[31] Lawrence A. Cremin, *The Republic and the School: Horace Mann on the Education of Free Men* (New York: Teachers College Press, 1957), 87.

[32] Tyack and Hansot, *Managers of Virtue,* 63–72.

Other concerns of common school advocates were organizational. First, to ensure educational uniformity and efficiency, these reformers promoted centralization and standardization. They worked for the consolidation of small school districts, instituting procedures for state supervision and regulation and transferring the control of schooling from private persons to the public sector. The position of state superintendent was created to oversee the education process, with superintendents at the city, district, and county levels serving as implementers. Local superintendents were responsible for visiting each school under their jurisdiction to monitor the content and quality of instruction. (Later, as schools became larger and their structures more complex, school principals assumed this task.)

During the early years of common schools, 300 or more students of all ages were taught simultaneously by a master teacher and several assistant teachers. Before long, however, children were being assigned to classes on the basis of age, marking the advent of *graded schooling.* Over time, these age groups were divided further, producing the educational model closest to that used in twentieth-century schools. Teachers in graded schools were supervised by a principal and his assistant.[33]

As with other aspects of American life, educational reformers looked to Europe for models, such as the instructional system developed by Joseph Lancaster (1778–1838) in England. His organizational approach to education appealed to Americans because, in addition to allowing large numbers of children to be taught at one time, it instilled the discipline and order desired in the changing industrial republic. The *Lancasterian system* (also known as the "monitorial" or "mutual" system) was a factorylike operation built on the notion that there was a time and a place for everything. Pedagogically the system emphasized recitation and memorization, and by using older students as monitors or teaching assistants, it allowed children to advance in their studies at their own pace.

A second European system that influenced American public education during these formative years was the child-centered pedagogy developed by Swiss educator Johann Heinrich Pestalozzi (1746–1827) and used extensively in Prussian schools. Pestalozzi believed that the learning process was set in motion when sense impressions, or *anschauungen,* the natural result of human perception, were received by the mind. Learning then unfolded gradually as mind or thought made these impressions clearer. Pestalozzi observed that when learning occurred naturally, without the aid of formal instruction, it was seamless, continuous, and sequential. Thus, he reasoned, teaching involved facilitating this process, particularly for underprivileged individuals whose living conditions appeared "to curtail the perfection of higher intellectual powers."[34]

Common schooling spread throughout the states, though many Americans opposed it.[35] Roman Catholics (primarily in the Northeast) were among the most resistant groups, and two Catholic schools were established in New York as alternatives to the public schools' pan-Protestant moral instruction. These first parochial institutions received state funding, because the separation between church and state had not yet been established.

---

[33] The masculine pronoun is appropriate because it conveys the organizational and administrative policies of common schools as a consequence of nineteenth-century thought about women and their role in society.

[34] Arthur Efland, "Art and Music in the Pestalozzian Tradition," in *Journal of Research in Music Education* (Fall 1983), 165–178.

[35] Kaestle, 136–182.

Later, when 1825 legislation in New York discontinued the allocation of state funds to support private schools, clergy and parents protested against double taxation. The issue became more heated and political. State officials eventually proposed establishing publically funded schools to be administered by Catholic church leaders, but opposition to the plan intensified Protestant-Catholic hostility. This and subsequent proposals failed because politicians and church administrators could not resolve their differences. Thus, the two education systems—Protestant free public schooling and Catholic parish schooling—developed side by side but separate.

Because southern resistance to public schooling was also strong, organized public schooling was virtually nonexistent in the South. Education there adhered to a variety of older forms: (1) private instruction for children from wealthy families; (2) religious and practical instruction in day schools, Sunday schools, "old field" schools, charity schools, academies, and colleges for the large proportion of children from middle-class families and a small proportion of poor children; and (3) little or no instruction for children of slaves or freemen. Most southern states passed laws forbidding slaves to receive academic instruction following slave revolts in the 1820s. This legislation perpetuated the illiteracy of slaves by limiting their education to carefully monitored religious training, and the situation worsened as abolitionist sentiment strengthened.

During the formative years of common schools, slavery became the primary source of conflict and divisiveness in American society. In fact, splits among the nation's largest religious groups—the Methodists, the Baptists, and the Presbyterians—were primarily attributable to the slavery question. These divisions were not initially or exclusively regional, but they had clearly become so by the middle to late 1850s. The Missouri Compromise (1820), the Compromise of 1850, the Fugitive Slave Act (1850), Harriet Beecher Stowe's *Uncle Tom's Cabin* (1852), and the Kansas-Nebraska Act of 1854 exacerbated escalating friction between North and South that eventually erupted in the Civil War.

Once the war ended, educational improvement was more urgent than in pre-war years because the conflict had completely unsettled American education. Schools and colleges had been used as soldiers' quarters or infirmaries, and numerous teachers from all educational levels had enlisted in the armed forces to support one side or the other. More important, Americans remained deeply divided. Supporters of public education sought once again to bridge differences by providing a common education for all citizens. In particular, Northerners who believed that war would have been averted if common schools had been a greater force in Southern states now promoted common schooling as the only way to reclaim the South. Nevertheless, educational access for all Southern children lagged far behind other parts of the country.

Music Education in Common Schools

While American leaders were reshaping general education prior to the Civil War, singing schools and musical societies remained popular, although regional tastes and needs varied. Among Southerners, singing schools and shape-note tune books gained popularity and were printed in large numbers. Northerners, on the other hand, were seeking a new musical challenge. Consequently, many educational reformers in the North developed early models of music instruction in general schooling. One of these educators, William C. Woodbridge (b. 1794), was not a musician, but after observing Swiss and German schools in which Pestalozzi's principles were being adapted and applied to music teaching, his efforts to reform American education, particularly in Connecticut, included support for vocal music instruction. Likewise, Elam Ives (1802–1864), a singing-school instructor and author, promoted music education. Ives was introduced to Pestalozzi's ideas by Woodbridge, and his subsequent publications and music teaching were grounded in Pestalozzian principles. Woodbridge, Ives, and others prepared the way for Lowell Mason (1792–1872), the man known as the "father of public school music."[36]

Mason was born into a prominent and musical family in Medfield, Massachusetts, where he attended singing school and became proficient on several instruments. By age sixteen he was directing the choir in one of Medfield's churches, and by age eighteen he was directing the city's band. In 1812 Mason moved to Savannah, Georgia, where he became a partner in a dry-goods firm and began offering singing schools for church choir members. Three years later he was hired as organist and choir director of Savannah's Independence Presbyterian Church. Mason also began composing during this time, and some of the anthems and hymns in his first published collection, the *Boston Handel and Haydn Society Collection of Church Music* (1821/1822), were his own. This collection established his reputation as a choirmaster and spokesman for church music reform.

When Mason returned to the North, he was elected president of Boston's Handel and Haydn Musical Society and served as director of two church choirs. Under his leadership, both choirs acquired national reputations for excellence in church music performance. Mason's musical life was not devoted entirely to church music, however. Children's music became a priority for him, and he relinquished the presidency of the musical society in 1832 to begin a vocal class for children at Bowdoin Street Church and to teach music in several of the city's private schools. The same year, Mason, with his colleague George James Webb and other local musicians, established the Boston Academy of Music, dedicated to improving the quality of church music and promoting general music education. Two years later, *The Manual of the Boston Academy of Music for Instruction in the Elements of Vocal Music on the System of Pestalozzi,* a translation of an earlier German publication, was published under Mason's name and became the official text for the academy's music teacher training courses.[37]

Boston Academy, the country's leading independent music education institution, offered instruction for adults and children, but its leaders were strongly in favor of music in common schools. Academy associates and other prominent citizens submitted two proposals to the Massachusetts School Board urging that vocal music instruction be made part of the primary school curriculum. Following the second of these proposals (1837), the board agreed to an experimental inclusion of vocal music at Hawes Primary School; Mason volunteered his services as instructor. In 1838 the board voted to include music in public elementary schools, marking the first time in American history that music was officially

---

[36] See Keene, 89–127; and Mark and Gary, 115–134.
[37] Mark and Gary, 125–130; and Keene, 106–113.

given a place in the school curriculum. From Boston to Cincinnati, other towns and cities gradually added music to their school programs. Boards of education sanctioned music study because, like other subjects, it helped to achieve moral, communal, physical, and educational goals.[38]

Developments in Vocal Music Pedagogy

With vocal music a required subject in primary schools, musicians began debating the relative merits of various instructional approaches. Singing schools had demonstrated the value of "singing by note," and the importance of this skill was never questioned by singing-school instructors or their students. Nor was it questioned during the late 1700s by the singing societies, whose performance of new European music required that singers be able to interpret the printed musical page. The teaching strategy most often used in both of these institutions involved repetition, drill, and memorization.

Then came Pestalozzi's child-oriented educational approach suggesting that musical sound precede music reading and that the meaning of music symbols should be derived from their function. In light of these ideas, musical instruction moved away from academic techniques toward an aural and singing-based pedagogy in which songs initially taught by rote were later used to demonstrate the meaning of musical terms and symbols. Under this instructional approach, school music consisted of "singing, and much of the song material was created for didactic purposes. The texts were frequently designed to impart secularized lessons drawn from Protestant Christian morality."[39]

This widely used *rote-song method* came under fire after the Civil War, when some educators urged that music instruction be more academic and skills-oriented. As a result, many of the graded[40] music books published during this period sought to provide a systematic and sequential method for developing music reading skill. The earliest of these was *Vocal Music Reader* (1861), a two-volume set for primary and grammar school children. Its author was Joseph Bird, a longstanding and outspoken opponent of the rote-song method whose pamphlet *To Teachers of Music* (1850) set forth concerns about the method.

Some years later, George B. Loomis' *First Steps in Music* (1868–1869) became the model for subsequent music texts. Early exercises in his first volume used a one-line staff,

---

[38] Mark and Gary, 141–153; and Keene, 113–120.

[39] Mark and Gary, *A History of American Music Education,* 168. In this way, song texts served a function similar to that of other instructional materials used in common schools. One of the most popular readers of this period provides an example. William Holmes McGuffey (1800–1873) designed his reading texts (published between 1836 and 1838) to develop a literate society that valued literature for leisure and self-education. An additional objective of these and similar publications—moral and ethical instruction—became more important and pronounced after the war. Thus, his introductory primer, speller, and graded readers used fables, readings about nature and history, and religious writings to convey lessons in morality and ethics. Although *McGuffey Readers* had been used widely in antebellum common schools, their popularity increased dramatically after the war. Between 1836 and 1922, approximately 122 million copies of these books were sold, with the largest single sales period from 1870 and 1890, when 60 million copies—nearly one-half the total—were sold.

[40] The term *graded* referred to the level of the institution (primary school, grammar school, and high school) rather than to divisions of learners within levels (first grade, second grade, and so forth). See Robert W. John, "Nineteenth Century Graded Vocal Series," *Journal of Research in Music Education* (Fall 1954), 103–118.

which was gradually extended to the traditional five-line staff. Loomis's second volume then used traditional notation to present unison songs and rounds, and the third volume introduced time signatures and included short two-part exercises harmonized primarily in thirds and sixths. These exercises were intended to develop music reading ability rather than improve students' musical taste or increase their music appreciation.

In spite of these publications, sequential music materials did not become popular until the last quarter of the century, mainly as the result of a series developed by Luther Whiting Mason (1828–1896). In 1857, Mason had become acquainted with *Hohmann's Practical Course,* or *The Practical Course of Instruction in Singing, Prepared on School Principles* (1856), an English translation of the music method developed by Christian Heinrich Hohmann (1811–1861) for use in German schools. Mason's influential *National Music Course* (written and published between 1870 and 1875) reflected Hohmann's influence. Mason believed that music reading should develop as language reading developed— with the aural preceding the written. His texts (also called *National Music Readers*) utilized this "rote before note" method extensively. Like compilers of early tune books and instructional manuals, Mason attempted to simplify music reading. First, he used tonic sol-fa, the movable do system developed in England by Sarah Anna Glover (1786–1867) and expanded by John Curwen (1816–1880).[41] This system introduced solmization by having students sing from a sol-fa tone ladder (a vertical arrangement of the first letters of each syllable do through ti) that conveyed relative pitch levels and relationships visually. Next, students moved to letter notation, which used the first letter of each syllable rather than traditional staff notation. Along with this, the first reader used a rhythm notation system much like that used by Tufts during the Colonial period: Duration was indicated by a system of punctuation marks and by the distance between printed syllables. Finally, the transfer from solmization to traditional musical notation was made in the second volume of the series via the C-major scale.

Mason's series revived debates about school music pedagogy because, according to many music educators, his texts posed serious problems. The method only developed music reading skill when taught by musicians or those trained to use the method. However, as there was a shortage of music specialists, classroom teachers were usually responsible for music instruction, and their students rarely progressed beyond rote learning. Consequently, as used in many classrooms, Mason's method was little more than group singing that entertained but resulted in minimal music reading ability. Because "school officials generally did not look with favor on . . . areas of study which tended strongly toward entertainment,"[42] the only recourse for music education advocates was to present music as "a 'scientific' subject with beneficial effects on mental training and health. On such a basis music was more favorably received as a school subject."[43] *The Normal Music Course* (1883), written by Hosea Edson Holt (1836–1898) and John Wheeler Tufts (1825–1908), offered this approach.

---

[41] This system replaced the fasola or four-note gamut system of solfege and shaped notes previously used by singing school instructors.

[42] Robert W. John, "Nineteenth Century Graded Vocal Series," in *Journal of Research in Music Education* (Fall 1954), 112.

[43] Ibid.

Holt and Mason had worked together in Boston after Holt was placed in charge of grammar school music there in 1869. Over time, however, Holt came to disagree with the rote procedures advocated in Mason's series. Like many of his colleagues, he believed that music education desperately needed an "academic" series that used high-quality repertoire to develop musical taste and musicality. Thus, Holt and Tufts' *Normal Music Course* became popular primarily because it required discipline and effort on the part of students. Like Mason's *National Music Course,* theirs was a graduated series of five readers, with three supplementary repertoire books (issued independently as *The Cecilian Series of Study and Song*) and charts. But in addition to this, the series enabled teachers to evaluate students' progress by testing their sight-singing abilities, as these were the foundation of the method.[44]

Promotion of instructional materials published during the postwar period usually involved training teachers to use the method. Toward the end of the century, music publishers began offering college credit for summer courses (music conventions) during which the authors of the materials they published taught teachers how to use the materials in the classroom. Conventions such as these led to the establishment of professional organizations in which teachers could discuss pedagogical matters and share ideas. Many such organizations were initially developed at the national level, but by 1850 professional teacher associations had been organized in most states.[45]

Perhaps the most influential national organization was the National Education Association (NEA), established in 1879. Music educators who were members of the NEA took an active role in its Department of Music Education (instituted in 1883), but the need for an autonomous music education organization became evident as school music programs and the number of music teachers and supervisors increased. When the San Francisco earthquake forced the NEA to cancel its 1906 convention, Philip C. Hayden, an active Department of Music Education member, invited thirty of his colleagues to a special meeting in Keokuk, Iowa, to discuss music education concerns. This session proved to be the initial meeting of the Music Supervisors National Conference (MSNC), although the organization's name and constitution were not adopted until its third annual meeting, in 1910.

THE PROGRESSIVE PERIOD (1880–1950)

Life changed rapidly from 1880 to 1910. Transatlantic communication restructured international relationships. The telephone transformed local communication and provided employment opportunities for women who, as operators, became known as "hello girls" and "Central." Artificial lighting altered lifestyles by extending hours for work and leisure. Photography, phonographs, and moving pictures extended the boundaries of reality and revised notions about past, present, and future. Amusement parks, complete with Ferris wheels and roller coasters, offered entertainment that made machinery a form of play as well as a pervasive aspect of work. Cast-iron stoves and furnaces resulted in larger homes,

[44] Ibid.
[45] Ibid.

although the number of occupants in most households decreased as Americans began separating the nuclear family from the extended family.[46]

The U.S. grew steadily from 1830 on, but between 1860 and 1910, the country's
rural population grew from 25,226,000 to 49,973,000, and its urban population increased
nearly 700 percent—from 6,126,000 to 41,998,000.[47] Nearly 30 percent of the country's
population lived west of the Mississippi River, and many of the new western communities
were primarily composed of native Europeans, Latin Americans, and Asians. Many native-
born Americans moved west, while others relocated in urban areas, which accounted for
almost half the nation's population by 1900. In addition, the Great Migration of southern
African Americans to the Northeast and Midwest that began just after the Civil War,
gained momentum between 1890 and 1910 and continued unabated for nearly six
decades.[48] In short, this sixty-year period (particularly the last twenty years of the nineteenth century) was one of transformation and the term "progressive" denotes the general
departure from tradition that characterized it.

American thought was greatly influenced by industry. Whereas concepts like hierar-
chical organization, specialization, efficiency, utility, mechanistic precision, and scientific
clarity had primarily been associated with factories, Americans now related them to social
aspects of life as well. More and more, society was seen as a complex system that could
be controlled and managed if it was scientifically analyzed and structured. Educational
changes that Horace Mann and others proposed in the 1830s and 1840s stemmed from a
belief that schooling had the power to change individuals and alter their interactions and
was, therefore, the key to societal well-being, prosperity, and progress. Progressive educators shared this faith in education, although they added another dimension, the scientific
study of human characteristics. Increasingly, responsibility for resolving societal problems
was given over to the schools and to science.

Developments in General Education

Until the late 1800s, compulsory attendance mandates had not been enforced, but given
the prevailing view that education played a crucial role in perpetuating republican unity,
prosperity, and freedom, voluntary compliance with attendance statutes was no longer seen
as viable. Capitalist leaders renewed their support for required school attendance and compulsory education, and by 1915, all states had enacted such regulations.[49] Children
throughout the country were bound by these laws, but the quality of schooling was uneven.
Common-school ideology had not overcome the beliefs that perpetuated segregated edu-

---

[46] See Thomas J. Schlereth, *Victorian America: Transformations in Everyday Life, 1876–1915* (New York: Harper Perennial, 1991).

[47] Richard Hofstadter, *The Age of Reform* (New York: Vintage Books, 1955), 174.

[48] See Nicholas Lehmann, *The Promised Land: The Great Black Migration and How it Changed America* (New York: Alfred A. Knopf, 1991).

[49] See Tyack and Hansot, 101–103.

cation. Legislation mandating separate schools for various ethnic groups was approved and enforced through the early 1900s. Most ethnic groups were forced to provide their own educational institutions at one time or another.[50]

Different treatment of African Americans had been institutionalized since colonial years. But in the late 1800s and early 1900s, there were those in black and white communities who fought openly against unequal educational opportunities. Booker T. Washington (1856–1915) and W.E.B. DuBois (1868–1963) were advocates for the education of African American citizens, although they disagreed about what the goals of this education should be and how these goals should be accomplished. Whereas Washington's "accommodationist" views seemed to favor some degree of racial separation, DuBois vehemently opposed compromise and was equally outspoken about existing racial inequities. Interestingly, both perspectives served to prolong resistance to integration, one by articulating the threat that equal educational opportunity represented to the status quo, and the other by condoning centuries-old segregationist ideas and practices.

Schools that were inhospitable to America's immigrant and African American populations remained nearly as hostile to Roman Catholics. Numerous Catholic children stayed away from public schools, which had become known as "Protestant" or "secular" schools among Catholic Americans. In 1884 Catholic church leaders decreed that every church without a parish school should establish one, and Catholic children were required to attend these schools unless they received official permission to do otherwise.

New Forms of Schooling

Boston's English Classical School had opened in 1821 as the first U.S. *high school*. Initially the high school curriculum resembled that of seventeenth- and eighteenth-century academies: It focused on academic training and offered few curricular options. But between 1880 and 1930, as enrollments increased by almost 50 percent each decade, educational leaders' efforts to make high school education useful for all students (especially the proportion that would not attend a university) led to *differentiated* or *tiered schooling*. Under this new curricular structure, high schools offered four courses of study. Decisions about which program students should follow were based on the students' aspirations, and, more important, on their natural abilities.[51] Whereas "equal opportunity" had previously meant equal access to the same experiences, it now meant equal access to appropriate experiences. Stated another way, equal opportunity meant allowing students the chance to

---

[50] See Lawrence A. Cremin, *American Education: The Metropolitan Experience, 1876–1980* (New York: Harper and Row, 1988), 251–255.

[51] The belief that intelligence was innate and essentially unalterable became more prevalent prior to World War I as psychology developed and scientific measurement increased. At the same time, social Darwinism and research studies conducted by Edward L. Thorndike (1842–1910) and others seemed to confirm that educational gains were more a function of genetic abilities than schooling. Choices among the four high school curricula (the *classical* curriculum, which included Latin and Greek; the *Latin-scientific* curriculum, requiring Latin; and the *modern language* and *English* programs, neither having a Latin requirement) were based in large measure on such notions.

prepare for occupations that were best suited to their character, abilities, and social status. The nature of students' education, then, was determined and often restricted by projections about their futures.

While high schools were becoming the dominant form of schooling for teenagers, the first American *junior high schools* were developed for seventh- and eight-grade students in New York in 1905. These intermediate schools received little public support until the Smith-Hughes Act of 1917 cited them as being important links in a system that prepared "human capital" for adult life. Junior high schools maximized educational efficiency by using vocational counseling to steer students into the most appropriate high school curriculum for their projected role in society. These projections were based at least in part on the results of intelligence tests, which were being used with increasing frequency in education.

The *kindergarten* spread quickly during the late 1800s and marked the revival of early-childhood programs that had existed during the earlier part of the century.[52] Its curriculum was designed to replace the dissipating influence of church, family, and community by preparing young children for formal elementary schooling. There were more than 200,000 kindergartens in the United States by the turn of the century, of which approximately 58 percent were housed in public schools.

Two additional forms of American schooling began during the late 1800s. *Supplementary schools* were specifically for children with special physical, social, or intellectual needs and remained a part of the United States' educational system well into the twentieth century. *Summer* or *vacation schools,* established in increasing numbers during this period, were intended to fill voids created by transformations in the family in much the same way as kindergartens.

Finally, several noninstructional additions to the school's functions provide the most concrete example of the degree to which these institutions were viewed as solutions to societal problems. School lunch programs, nurses, showers and baths, and playgrounds all date from this period. Each became part of the educational structure as reformers attempted to realize America's potential through its young people.

Instrumental Music in Schools

Military band members had returned to civilian life after the Civil War hoping to make a living through music. One of these men, Irish immigrant and bandsman Patrick S. Gilmore (1829–1892), generated considerable interest in band performances.[53] Gilmore, who had directed military bands during the war, organized several touring instrumental ensembles

---

[52] The kindergarten originated in Germany during the late 1830s and early 1840s. Friedrich Froebel (1752–1852) developed kindergartens to facilitate social development, viewing them as "a garden of children to be cultivated in the same manner as plants." Like Pestalozzi, Froebel preferred the nurturing approach used by female teachers for developing the "divine spirit" in every child, thereby leading to social harmony. See Spring, 163–165.

[53] See Keene, 283–285; and Mark and Gary, 262–263.

that performed in amusement parks. But perhaps Gilmore's most impressive accomplishments were his mass concerts known as "Peace Jubilees," the first of which was presented in 1869 and included choruses of adults and children totalling more than 20,000 singers. Gilmore's second jubilee, presented in 1872, included the Fisk Jubilee Singers and violinist Ole Bull, along with a number of European ensembles.

John Philip Sousa (1854–1932), a younger contemporary of Gilmore, was equally successful. His bands not only achieved popularity with audiences in the United States but gained worldwide renown.[54] Later, when colleges and public schools began offering instrumental instruction, Sousa was one of their strongest and most influential supporters.

String ensembles were also common during the postwar period, although they were eclipsed somewhat by bands. The orchestra's popularity grew through men like professional violinist Theodore Thomas (1825–1905), who organized the Theodore Thomas Orchestra in 1862 and toured the United States with this ensemble for a number of years. From 1877 to 1891 Thomas served as director of the New York Philharmonic Orchestra, after which he founded the Chicago Symphony Orchestra.[55]

By the 1930s, professional concert bands had given way to jazz ensembles whose new music was better suited to popular dances of the 1920s and 1930s. Moreover, amusement parks and beaches, previously popular sites for band concerts, were somewhat less frequented as automobiles opened new ways to spend leisure time. In addition, musical performances could be heard at home via radio broadcasts.

Nevertheless, concert bands and professional orchestras had so increased the public's interest in music that the period from approximately 1920 through the early 1940s was one of rapid expansion in public school music. Group instruction on instruments, for example, had been offered in parts of the country prior to the Civil War, but at the turn of the century these classes gained wide acceptance in public schools.

During the first quarter-century Albert Mitchell, supervisor of music in Boston, and his colleagues Charles Farnsworth and Paul Stoeving explored the possibility of establishing public school orchestras. Once again, a European program provided the model. Just after the turn of the century, these men observed string classes in Maidstone, England. Then in 1911, when Mitchell returned to Boston after a study leave to observe the Maidstone program more closely, he organized after-school violin classes for groups of sixteen to twenty students. These classes were so successful that they became part of the regular school day. Subsequently, Mitchell facilitated the organization of other schools orchestras by writing and publishing his *Violin Class Method,* which replaced English materials he had been using.[56]

Interest in school orchestras continued to grow, although bands were more common and popular. By emphasizing the extramusical and societal benefits of these ensembles, music educators and school administrators garnered substantial support for them, especially during World War I. As a result, bands had acquired an official place in school

[54] Ibid.
[55] Mark and Gary, 261–262.
[56] See Keene, 281–282, 290.

schedules by 1923 and held regular rehearsals under the direction of trained and salaried, though usually uncertified, musicians.

Music Appreciation Classes

As access to musical performances expanded, a new concern surfaced for music educators. Throughout U.S. history the public's interest and involvement in music implied some appreciation of the art form even though instruction usually focused on performance and reading music. Around the turn of the century many educators began to wonder whether traditional instruction went far enough, since it did not include information about music history, musical structure, and the like. They were also concerned that existing modes of instruction failed to reach large numbers of potential concertgoers and that those who did attend concerts did not know enough about music.

Frances Elliott Clark (1860–1958) was the most influential music appreciation advocate of this period.[57] Like many of her peers, she received early music training in a singing school and was, for a time, a singing-school instructor. After being widowed in 1880, Clark decided to become a teacher. Over the next sixteen years, she was graduated from normal school,[58] studied music and voice in public school and privately, completed the Ginn Institute course for music supervisors in Detroit, and taught music for two years in Illinois schools.

In 1896 while teaching in Iowa, Clark began preparing short talks about music to present to her choral ensembles before rehearsals. It was as supervisor of music in Milwaukee, however, that she established her reputation in teaching. Milwaukee was a musical town, although little had been done there to promote school music. Upon arriving in 1903 Clark began working with teachers to organize general music instruction for all grades, especially elementary schools. Under her leadership, general music instruction began in the first eight grades of Milwaukee's schools shortly after her arrival. She also introduced remedial singing and ear-training programs in kindergarten classes throughout the city. These soon became popular in other cities as well.

It was also in Milwaukee that Clark began her music appreciation work in earnest. Recognizing the potential of the relatively new Victor Talking Machine for music instruction, she convinced two principals to let her teach trial classes in their buildings using the device. These experimental lessons were successful, so she extended this innovative work to more groups of students. Before long, her idea was recognized nationally and ultimately led to her appointment as director of the first educational department at Victor Talking Machine Company. While working at Victor, Clark developed instructional materials that augmented or improved existing music instruction and made music classes possible in schools where it had not previously been offered. Largely because of her efforts, the educational uses of recorded music became widely acknowledged.

[57] Ibid., 244–270.

[58] The term *normal school* "orginated in France and meant that teachers should be trained to perform according to high standards or *norms*." These institutions gradually replaced seminaries and teachers' institutes. Carl F. Kaestle, *Pillars of the Republic: Common Schools and American Society, 1780–1860* (New York: Hill and Wang, 1983), 129.

Music Contests and Music Performance

Several types of music contests became commonplace as music educators capitalized on the competitive spirit that ran high in the United States immediately before and after World War I. The first contests were held in 1912 in Kansas, where music supervisors sponsored an All-Kansas Music Competition Festival. Public response was enthusiastic, as it was for a similar event held in North Dakota approximately seven years later. The success of these and other city or regional instrumental contests prompted the first national band competition in 1923. A contest movement for high school vocal ensembles also began during this period, with the first statewide competition held in Kansas in 1914.

Not all music competitions instituted during the war years were performance oriented. Music appreciation courses set the stage for the enormously popular music memory contest movement, which lasted approximately twenty-five years.[59] Radio programs helped the growth of this movement by featuring works slated for future competitions. Similarly, professional instrumental ensembles programmed these selections during their concert season. The contests were musical guessing games. Children worked together to prepare for the contests, drilling each other on the compositions by humming the themes. Some of these young people came to know, recognize, and identify as many as fifty compositions by title and composer during a single contest period.

In spite of this popularity, many music educators questioned the merits of these contests, contending that participants learned little about music as an art form. Some educators tried to increase the educational value of contests by including historical and descriptive notes in packets that were sent out to publicize the contest selections. Others included contest selections in music appreciation lessons they taught prior to a contest period. Nevertheless, music memory contests gradually dwindled during the late 1930s and early 1940s.

General Education in the Late Progressive Period

During the early 1900s, several ideas combined to have far-reaching effects on life in the U.S., and these ideas' impact on public education reflects the extent to which national leaders embraced them as ways of sustaining and improving American society in the midst of rapid expansion and industrialization. *Scientific management* or *Taylorism,* was a theory of mass production and industrial management developed by Frederick Winslow Taylor (1856–1915) as a result of time and motion studies he conducted between 1881 and 1893 while working at the Midvale Steel Plant in Philadelphia, Pennsylvania. Taylor believed that the primary problems of American industry were disorganization and inadequate supervision of labor. His Midvale studies convinced him and others that there was a cost effective and time efficient way of performing every task. Under Taylorism, the supervisor's or manager's job was to discover these methods and teach them to workers they supervised. In turn, these workers would do more work in less time, enabling industry to

---

[59] Keene, 263–269.

earn greater profits without spending more money.[60] Taylor did not invent assembly-line and mass-production methods, but he perfected, rationalized, and promoted them. Moreover, by "vesting direction in the experts at the top and deskilling work at the bottom,"[61] Taylorism accelerated national movement toward professionalizing teachers and school officials and bureaucratizing educational administration.

Professional expansion in the U.S. began just after the Civil War but escalated in the wake of the farming and industrial depressions of the early 1890s. Between 1890 and 1910, the number of Americans involved in professions such as divinity, medicine, law, engineering, and education rose from 944,000 to 1,758,000. During this period, teacher training programs moved from normal schools to teachers' colleges and emphasized pedagogy and subject matter rather than scholarship.[62] The education received by prospective teachers was quite different from that received by a growing number of individuals enrolled in school administration and supervision curricula at various teachers' colleges, however. Training programs for public school administrators were primarily devoted to courses in the executive, financial, organizational, and legal aspects of schools rather than to educational philosophy, pedagogy, scholarship, or critical examination of educational problems in twentieth-century American society.[63]

Public education in most cities during the early 1800s was run by small school boards made up of lay people from the community, but by the mid-1800s. as annexation and immigration generated more cities with larger local school boards, schools were grouped into wards or districts with elected superintendents to oversee the operations of local school boards. Initially, many of these superintendents and board members were prominent citizens and business people in their communities; they were non-educators who were interested in the schooling of youth in their community. Before long, however, upper-level administrative positions in education and seats on school board fell prey to politicians who freely exchanged favors to special interest groups for votes. To reduce political corruption, wards and districts were consolidated into city school systems, and a small board of the "best" people (known then as "the educational trust") were elected by nonpartisan voting and placed in charge of the system. During this period, then, public education in America changed "from a part-time, lay-controlled labor of love"[64] to a hierarchically organized bureaucracy. Graduates from college programs in educational administration and leaders in industry were trained and experienced in effective management and gradually assumed responsibility for the nation's schools, although the bulk of the responsibility for school governance rested with school administrators.[65]

---

[60] Ray Marshall and Marc Tucker, *Thinking for a Living: Education and the Wealth of Nations* (New York: Basic Books, 1992), 5; and Spring, 234–235.

[61] Tyack and Hansot, *Managers of Virtue,*158.

[62] See Cremin, *American Education: The Metropolitan Experience, 1876–1980,* 492–502.

[63] Spring, 227–238.

[64] Douglas E. Mitchell, "Governance of Schools," in *Encyclopedia of Educational Research,* 6th ed., ed. Marvin C. Alkin (New York: Macmillan Publishing Company, 1992).

[65] See Cremin, *American Education: The Metropolitan Experience,* 225–226; Spring, 227–238; Tyack and Hansot, 105–114; and Douglas E. Mitchell, "Governance of Schools."

This alliance between education and industry was profitable for the country because students who left public schools were well prepared to be productive members of an industrial society. The alliance broke down under the economic difficulties of the Depression years, however. School officials were pressured by business people, politicians, and society at large to cut expenditures and were criticized as being impractical when they refused to do so. In addition, outspoken citizens maintained that by trying to accommodate the needs of the growing numbers of American school children, educational administrators were fostering "soft" pedagogy, overemphasizing vocational training, neglecting character formation, making excessive work demands, and being too strict on students.[66]

School administrators were also at odds with teachers. Perhaps because they believed teachers knew little about the business of schooling, administrators felt justified in lowering teachers' salaries even though they refused to cut instructional programs. Rapport between administrators and teachers deteriorated so much that the American Federation of Teachers (AFT) was organized to fight for some measure of security for teachers and against poor working conditions, growing administrative regulation, and inadequate pay.[67]

As criticism of the educational system and concern about educating young people intensified, the U.S. government assumed a more active role in education, which generated tension between education and government that would persist into the 1960s. First Franklin D. Roosevelt in 1935 instituted the National Youth Administration (NYA), which paid students to return to school. During NYA's first year, high school students received $6 per month, and college students whose parents were receiving relief assistance received $15. Roosevelt's second youth education program, the Civilian Conservation Corps (CCC), began in 1933. Young men enrolled in CCC camps lived in a military-like environment, awakening to reveille at 6:00 a.m., having breakfast and doing some physical exercise, then spending most of the day engaged in activities such as fighting fires, building bridges, clearing trails, and planting trees. The teenagers could also attend evening vocational, remedial, and general education classes. These New Deal youth programs ended during World War II, partly because the domestic war effort helped to alleviate many youth problems by providing jobs.[68]

Toward the end of the war, attention shifted from war concerns to anticipation of postwar problems, among which was the role of formal education. Changes were seen as necessary, but what these changes should be, how they should be brought about, and to what end were pressing questions. These concerns, coupled with declines in high school enrollment and skepticism about the utility of existing high school curricula, suggested the need for programs attractive enough to reduce dropout rates while preparing students for adult life in the work world. The solution was "life adjustment education," which developed vocational and civic skills, communication and group interaction skills, and general readiness for home living. In addition to academic instruction, schools offered courses in driver education, home economics, and other "life situation" or "area of living" courses,

---

[66] See Spring, 256.

[67] See Spring, 225–257 and 259–282; and Marshall and Tucker, *Thinking for a Living,* 13–27.

[68] See Spring, 272–282; and Cremin, *American Education: The Metropolitan Experience,* 311–314.

which led some educators and societal leaders to begin calling for educational reform of a trend they considered anti-intellectual.[69]

THE SPACE AND TECHNOLOGY PERIOD (1950–1980)

The Cold War and Civil Rights

Whereas in 1880 just before the beginning of this progressive period, the U.S. ranked third in the world economy, it became the world's largest and wealthiest exporter by 1926, producing half of the world's steel, crude oil, and electricity and 80 percent of its automobiles. By the end of the progressive era in 1950, America's worth had grown from approximately $334 billion to just over $700 billion so that during this seventy-year period, the U.S. became the world's leading economic power.[70]

The United States was seemingly secure economically, industrially, and militarily. An abundance of high-paying jobs and governmental assistance programs such as the Serviceman's Readjustment Act (the G.I. Bill of Rights, 1944) afforded numerous citizens the opportunity to improve their socioeconomic status and acquire possessions. Apartment and tenement dwellers moved into private homes as prewar homeowners headed for residences in rapidly developing suburban areas. The proportion of families with incomes under $3,000 fell from 46 percent in 1947 to 20 percent in 1959, while the proportion of families with incomes of between $7,000 and $10,000 rose from 5 percent to 20 percent.[71]

The country prospered even as its relations with the Soviet Union became more strained. America's bombing of Hiroshima and Nagasaki in 1945, the Soviet Union's 1949 testing of its own atomic bomb (dubbed "Joe One" by Americans), and renewed discussion about more powerful hydrogen weaponry generated considerable anxiety about the future. For the next fifteen years or more, air-raid drills were common occurrences in schools and businesses, and many families constructed underground bomb shelters, stocked with canned goods and other emergency supplies in the event of war. These concerns were compounded by growing anxiety about long-range economic effects that the war might have. Americans lived in fear of another depression.

In its effort to cope with uncertainty, the country turned inward. Nationally, what one writer terms this *domestic ideology*[72] was manifested most notably in McCarthyism, a campaign against communism, the "Red Menace." Fears of communist infiltration of

---

[69] See Herbert M. Kliebard, *The Struggle for the American Curriculum: 1893–1958,* reprint ed. (New York: Routledge, 1991), 240–270.

[70] Ray Marshall and Marc Tucker, *Thinking for a Living: Education and the Wealth of Nations* (New York: Basic Books, 1992), 3, 31.

[71] Loren Baritz, *The Good Life: The Meaning of Success for the American Middle Class* (New York: Alfred A. Knopf, 1989), 184.

[72] Elaine Tyler May maintains that domestic ideology (or domestic containment) emerged during the Cold War era as America's "key to security": Potentially harmful forces—whether political, domestic, or personal—could be disarmed if they were limited to or "contained within a clearly defined sphere of influence." See May, *Homeward Bound: American Families in the Cold War Era* (Basic Books, 1988), for an in-depth discussion of this theory and various manifestations of domestic containment in America during the fifties.

American government had initially surfaced during World War I, and Cold War uncertainty revived and intensified them. The United States' susceptibility to these fears, particularly between 1945 and 1949, resulted in the most massive and inflammatory anticommunist movement in U.S. history. Joseph R. McCarthy (1908–1957), a Wisconsin senator, became the icon of a campaign that began with President Harry S. Truman's investigations of government employees and escalated into a national obsession. For McCarthy and others, Roosevelt's policies had initiated a downward spiral in morals and a dangerous erosion of American ideals. To prevent socialist ideas from further infecting society, these citizens set about identifying and "containing" those who supported communism or even liberalism.

One theory is that this "domestic ideology" led to widespread dependence on people who became recognized as authorities on everything from raising children to saving marriages and a plethora of other personal problems. Dr. Benjamin Spock's *Baby and Child Care* and Norman Vincent Peale's *The Power of Positive Thinking* became best-sellers during this era when "experts took over the role of psychic healer" and assumed the "much broader and more important role of directing the behavior, goals, and ideals of normal people."[73]

The image of the ideal American family also developed during these years. Americans sought security and stability in the nuclear family. Home and family mattered more to most people than community. In addition, birthrates rose to a twentieth-century high as a generation of Americans who married younger and remained married longer produced the 1950s "baby boom."

Technology added to the forces transforming life in the United States, and consumerism, spurred by the postwar economy, swept the country. Automobiles, refrigerators, and washing machines became symbols of a burgeoning middle class, as did a variety of other conveniences and devices. One of the most important of these was television. Whereas the first half of the 1900s had been the age of radio and cinema, this was the era of television broadcasting. From 1946 to 1950, the number of commercial stations grew from 30 to 104, and households with TV sets increased from 8,000 in 1946 to 5 million in 1950.[74]

Over time, television broadcasting combined with America's visibility and status to play an important role in domestic and international affairs. With this new medium, community or local events and issues became immediately widely public. Television portrayed vivid images of "the American dream" as realized by the country's affluent citizens. It also illuminated how the dream was being "deferred," as Langston Hughes wrote,[75] for a significant proportion of the population, primarily as a result of racism and widening socio-economic differences. Technology made it impossible to avoid or deny domestic inequities. It became clear to many that America's continued influence as a symbol of freedom depended on resolving internal conflicts.

[73] Joseph Veroff, Richard A. Kulka, and Elizabeth Douvan, *The Inner American: A Self-Portrait from 1957–1976.* (New York: Basic books, 1981), quoted in May, 27.

[74] Lawrence A. Cremin, *American Education: The Metropolitan Experience, 1876–1980* (New York: Harper and Row, 1988), 357.

[75] This reference is taken from Langston Hughes' poem "Harlem," from his collection *Montage of a Dream Deferred* (New York; Knopf, 1951).

Prior to the 1950s most minority children in the United States were educated separately from white children. The Fourteenth Amendment made it illegal to deny citizens an equal education, but the term *equal* had never meant *integrated*. The Supreme Court's ruling in *Plessy v. Ferguson* (1896) made it clear that so long as separate facilities were the same, they were legal. Consequently, when deciding cases related to educational separation, district courts routinely determined that separate schooling did not breach minority children's rights because the education they were receiving was equal to that received by their white peers.

Oliver Brown's suit against the Topeka, Kansas, Board of Education on behalf of his eight-year-old daughter was one of five such cases jointly appealed to the Supreme Court in the early 1950s.[76] These cases raised critical questions about American educational practices, but they were also the means by which Thurgood Marshall (1908–1993), an attorney for the National Association for the Advancement of Colored People (NAACP), and his colleagues intended to attack the heart of American racism: the earlier separate-but-equal Plessy decision. These attorneys realized that, just as *Plessy* condoned (or at least did not prohibit) separate educational facilities, it also sustained Jim Crow practices that persisted throughout the country, particularly in southern states.

Newly appointed Justice Earl Warren (1891–1974) also recognized that confronting segregation in schools meant confronting the *Plessy* decision. Furthermore, he knew that given the controversial nature of the case, the court had to be united in its decision regardless of its direction; there must be no question about its ruling. Warren therefore set about securing a unanimous decision, which he presented to the American public on May 17, 1954. The Supreme Court ruled that separate education facilities were by nature unequal and that children subjected to such schooling were being deprived of equal protection under the law, as guaranteed by the Fourteenth Amendment. One year after this ruling, with school districts continuing to resist desegregation, the Supreme Court underscored its mandate by requiring that districts with separate schooling implement integregation measures "with all deliberate speed."

These mandates notwithstanding, change occurred slowly. In 1955 Rosa Parks, a black seamstress, was arrested when she refused to relinquish her seat to a white male patron on a crowded Montgomery, Alabama, bus. Subsequent nonviolent protests and demonstrations led by Martin Luther King, Jr. (1929–1968) met with such violence that for more than a decade, American and international news media were filled with ugly and virulent images of a country once again at war with itself.

Ultimately the Civil Rights Act that had been drafted under President John F. Kennedy (1917–1963) prior to his assassination became law under his successor, Lyndon B. Johnson (1908–1973), in 1964. Various parts of this legislation initiated or strengthened federal regulations related to voting rights for African Americans, discrimination in schools, unfair or biased employment practices, and separate public facilities. The Educational Opportunities Act of 1964 (under which the Job Corps and Head Start were estab-

---

[76] *Brown v. Board of Education* was filed on direct appeal and was heard along with *Briggs v. Elliott* (Clarendon County, South Carolina), *Davis v. Prince Edward County* (Virginia), *Gebhart v. Belton* (Delaware), and *Bolling v. Sharpe* (District of Columbia).

lished) and the Elementary and Secondary Act (ESEA, 1965) were initiated as part of Johnson's 1960s "War on Poverty" and provided large-scale federal aid to public schools. Numerous federally funded categorical programs were established to redress educational and societal inequities. In particular, Title I of ESEA aimed to improve schooling for low-achieving students in low-income neighborhoods and received the greatest amount of federal dollars. Financial support attached to these programs was frequently used as leverage over states and school districts that were slow to comply with federal mandates.

A year after the Civil Rights Act and eleven years after *Brown v. Board of Education,* more than 75 percent of the country's southern school districts and numerous schools throughout the nation remained segregated, but equality movements in the United States continued. The 1960s were punctuated with civil rights campaigns on behalf of Hispanic Americans, women, Native Americans, religious groups, and other minorities that no longer regarded their status as fixed. In the wake of civil rights legislation for African Americans, numerous grassroots efforts were organized to secure equitable rights and opportunities for minority populations.

Schooling in the Post-World War II United States

The speed with which American life and world situations changed following World War II led to a general agreement that educational changes were imperative. National security was of immediate concern as was preparing a new generation of scientists, engineers, and mathematicians to ensure that America did not fall behind in the nuclear arms race. Although the Selective Service Act (1917) virtually guaranteed national preparedness for war, there was growing pressure for universal military training. But this would prevent many academically gifted young men from completing high school and attending college. James B. Conant (1893–1978), chemist and distinguished educator, and Vannevar Bush (1890–1974), developer of the first electronic analog computer, were two of many who voiced concern about the threat that such a policy presented to American research and advancement. Following open hearings debating universal training, Congressional amendments in 1951 gave young men the option of serving in the armed forces or going to college.

This legislation increased college enrollment in spite of concern that high schools were not preparing students for college study. Accusations of anti-intellectualism flew: Some people attributed what they perceived as educational inadequacies to "communist" teachers and "socialist" instructional materials, whereas some educators faulted the high school's "life adjustment" curriculum. Then the Soviet Union's October 1957 launching of the world's first earth-orbiting satellite, Sputnik I, signified that warnings and fears were well-founded. Schools and educators were attacked from all sides.

> The Sputnik was more than a shock to American national vanity: it brought an immense amount of attention to bear on the consequences of anti-intellectualism in the school system and in American life at large. Suddenly the national distaste for intellect appeared to be not just a disgrace but a hazard to survival. . . . Cries of protest against the slackness of American education, hitherto raised only by a small number of educational critics, were now taken

up by television, mass magazines, businessmen, scientists, politicians, admirals, and university presidents, and soon swelled into a national chorus of self-reproach.[77]

Concern about national security and the country's status as a world power prompted the federal government to take action. During the decade following Sputnik I, national expenditures for education rose tenfold, to account for approximately 10 percent of schooling costs. Congress immediately passed the National Defense Education Act (NDEA) in 1958, designed to improve curricula and instruction in mathematics, science, and foreign languages. In addition, the United State Office of Education's Cooperative Research Branch funded more than 400 research projects totaling in excess of $40 million.

Music Education after Sputnik

Even though many decision makers viewed nonacademic courses as curricular frills, school music benefitted from post-Sputnik educational expenditures.[78] One reason was that as emphasis shifted to academic subjects, educators and organizations in various disciplines cautioned against stressing academic or intellectual achievement at the expense of artistic and creative development. In addition, some educational, philanthropic, and governmental organizations shared a concern about music's role in a technological society and consequently invested in projects designed to improve and promote music instruction.

The first of these was the Young Composers Project, established in 1959 and funded by the Ford Foundation, that placed young composers in schools as composers-in-residence. Then in 1963 the Music Educators National Conference (MENC) administered a second, larger grant from the Ford Foundation, organizing workshops, seminars, and pilot programs to increase teachers' understanding of contemporary composition. This expanded form of the Young Composers Project was called the Contemporary Music Project for Creativity in Music Education (CMP).

By 1968, seventy-seven composers had been placed in public schools, and over the next five years, MENC and the Ford Foundation jointly funded the project. When CMP ended in 1973, it had accomplished its primary objectives of (1) synthesizing and focusing contemporary musical activities, (2) making the music education profession receptive to innovation and change, and (3) heightening music's relevance in contemporary society.

The Yale Seminar on Music Education, funded by the United States Office of Education, took place at Yale University in June 1963. Concern about arts education as voiced by members of President Kennedy's Panel on Educational Research and Development (an outgrowth of the National Science Foundation's success during the early post-Sputnik years) led to this two-week gathering where thirty-one music scholars and professional

---

[77] Richard Hofstadter, *Anti-Intellectualism in American Life* (New York, Vintage Books, 1962), 5–7. Before providing several definitions for the term *anti-intellectualism,* Hofstadter generally defines it as "a resentment and suspicion of the life of the mind and of those who are considered to represent it; and a disposition constantly to minimize the value of that life."

[78] See Michael L. Mark, *Contemporary Music Education,* 2d ed. (New York: Schirmer Books, 1986).

musicians met to formulate recommendations for improving music education. An important outcome of this seminar was the Juilliard Repertory Project. Musicians joined forces to research, field test, and compile vocal and instrumental compositions suitable for kindergarten through sixth grade. The result of their efforts, the Juilliard Repertory Library, was published by Canyon Press of Ohio.

Perhaps the most important music education meeting of this period was, in part, the profession's response to the minor role that music educators played in the Yale Seminar's initial phases. This meeting, now known as the Tanglewood Symposium,[79] was convened by the Music Educators National Conference in cooperation with the Theodore Presser Foundation, the Berkshire Music Center, and the School of Fine and Performing Arts of Boston University. For two weeks during the summer of 1967, a group of musicians and educators, corporate leaders, sociologists, scientists, foundation administrators, government officials, and others met at the Boston Symphony Orchestra's summer residence to (1) discuss music in American society, (2) assess the function of music in schools and other educational institutions,[80] (3) increase awareness of music's potential contributions to post-industrial American culture, and (4) speculate about cooperative efforts that might increase the effectiveness of music and musicians in society. Papers published in the March and April issues of *Music Educators Journal* were the basis for discussions about music education philosophy, pedagogy, repertoire, creativity, technology, curriculum, and assessment. Subsequently, a summary of the symposium's recommendations was published as the Tanglewood Declaration, a philosophical statement justifying music's place in a technological society and setting forth goals and strategies for general music education.

MENC's Goals and Objectives Project (the GO Project) began in 1969 as a first step toward achieving the Tanglewood Symposium's recommendations. GO formulated a prioritized list of thirty-five objectives that, when attained, would expand the breadth, depth, and quality of music education. These goals and objectives guided MENC's work through the 1970s.

Finally, the Manhattanville Music Curriculum Program (MMCP) was funded by the Arts and Humanities Program of the U. S. Department of Education. This five-year project (1965–1970) sought to devise a comprehensive music curriculum that was expressive, creative, and relevant to daily life rather than being academic, skills-oriented, and technical. MMCP formulators developed a tightly structured program that involved students in all phases of music, from performing and analyzing to creating and evaluating.[81]

Public school music programs also benefitted from what was perhaps the most influential general education seminar of this period—the Woods Hole (Massachusetts) Conference of 1959. This ten-day meeting focused on improving education in science, but the thirty-five psychologists, educators, historians, physicists, biologists, and mathematicians

---

[79] Robert A. Choate, ed., *Documentary Report of the Tanglewood Symposium* (Washington, DC: Music Educators National Conference, 1968).

[80] Tanglewood Conference attendees adopted a broad view of "educational institutions" that included churches, social and community organizations, and mass media.

[81] See Ronald B. Thomas, *MMCP Synthesis: A Structure for Music Education* (Washington DC: U. S. Office of Education, V–008; 6–1999, n.d.); reprint New York: Media Materials, Inc., n.d.

in attendance spent much of their time examining the general nature of teaching and learning. Specifically, they discussed the implications of instruction that emphasized the structure of a subject so that an understanding of its fundamental ideas could be grasped as early as possible during the educational process.

A pedagogical idea formulated during these discussions was the *spiral curriculum*. Under this curricular design, young students would learn about and use basic concepts of subject matter that would be revisited at subsequent levels and built on until students had "grasped the full formal apparatus that goes with them."[82] Many general music instruction materials and teacher aids developed and published in the United States after Woods Hole, particularly those for elementary education, were structured on this notion. Moreover, a number of general music pedagogies that were developed in other countries and became popular in America during the 1950s and 1960s also incorporate aspects of the spiral curriculum. These instructional methods are discussed in detail later in the text.

STUDY AND DISCUSSION QUESTIONS

1. Cite at least three reasons why singing schools remained such a vital part of American life for so long. Consider such issues as (a) why the schools were developed, (b) how they were organized, and (c) what life was like during the period in which they flourished.

2. Name one music education approach used during the national, progressive, and space and technology periods discussed in this chapter that was as influential in that era as singing schools were during the 1700s and early 1800s. Compare this music education approach with singing schools in light of your responses to Question 1.

3. Prepare an oral or written report about one of the following persons listed. Your presentation should discuss the person's ideas about education and explain ways in which the person's ideas were innovative or traditional at the time they were introduced.

    Peter Dykema (1873–1951)   John Amos Comenius (1592–1671)
    Noah Webster (1758–1848)   Mary M. Bethune (1875–1955)
    Jane Addams (1860–1935)   Elizabeth Peabody (1804–1894)

4. List at least three recurring themes or issues in general education from colonial days through 1980. Consider the following as you formulate a response: (a) societal, cultural, or philosophical factors leading up to or resulting from each theme; (b) important dates, places, people, and publications associated with each theme; and (c) immediate and long-range effects of each theme each time it appeared.

5. For each of the four major periods from the colonial period through 1980, cite one change in music education that can be *directly* linked to events or trends in society or general education. Then cite one change that was an *indirect* result of societal or educational events.

6. It is often said that musical composition and performance practices in any historical period reflect broader societal and cultural trends. Can the same be said about music edu-

[82] Ibid., 13.

cation practices? Cite and discuss music education practices used in any three major periods to support your answer.

7. Discuss similarities and differences among music education approaches used during the colonial period, the 1930s, and 1940s and in your own schooling experiences.

8. For two of the pre-1950s periods discussed in this chapter, select one influential person in general or music education. Summarize this person's educational perspective, then speculate on how the person would view general and music education in 1980.

REFERENCES AND RECOMMENDED SOURCES

ALDERFER, EVERETTE GORDON.   *The Ephrata Commune: An Early American Counterculture.* Pittsburgh: University of Pittsburgh Press, 1985.

BAILYN, BERNARD.   *The Ideological Origins of the American Revolution.* Enlarged ed. Cambridge, MA: Belknap Press, 1992.

BARITZ, LOREN.   *The Good Life: The Meaning of Success for the American Middle Class.* New York: Alfred A. Knopf, 1989; reprint, New York: Harper and Row, 1990.

BIRGE, EDWARD BAILEY.   *History of Public School Music in the United States.* New and augmented ed. Washington, DC: Music Educators National Conference, 1926.

BRUNER, JEROME S.   *The Process of Education.* Cambridge, MA: Harvard University Press, 1977.

BURNS, JAMES MACGREGOR, AND STEWART BURNS.   *The Pursuit of Rights: A People's Charter.* New York: Vintage Books, 1991.

CHASE, GILBERT.   *America's Music: From the Pilgrims to the Present.* With a foreword by Richard Crawford and a discographical essay by Williams Brooks. Revised 3d ed. Urbana: University of Illinois Press, 1992.

CHOATE, ROBERT A., ed. *Documentary Report of the Tanglewood Symposium.* Washington, DC: Music Educators National Conference, 1968.

COLWELL, RICHARD.   "Education in Music: United State of America, Schools." In *New Grove Dictionary of Music and Musicians.* Ed. by Stanley Sadie. London: Macmillan, 1980.

CREMIN, LAWRENCE A.   *American Education: The Colonial Experience, 1607–1783.* New York: Harper and Row, 1970.

———.   *American Education: The National Experience, 1783–1876.* New York: Harper and Row, 1980.

———.   *American Education: The Metropolitan the Experience, 1876–1980.* New York: Harper and Row, 1988.

———.   *The Republic and the School: Horace Mann on the Education of Free Men.* New York: Teachers College Press, 1957.

DU BOIS, W. E. B.   *The Souls of Black Folk.* Introduction by Henry Louis Gates Jr. New York: Bantam Books, 1989.

EFLAND, ARTHUR.   "Art and Music in the Pestalozzian Tradition." In *Journal of Research in Music Education* (Fall 1983): 165–178.

FRANKLIN, BENJAMIN.   "A Practical Theology." In *The Autobiography and Other Writings.* Selected and edited by L. Jesse Lemisch. New York: New American Library, 1961.

———.   "Proposals Relating to the Education of Youth in Pennsylvania." In *The Autobiography and Other Writings.* Selected and edited by L. Jesse Lemisch. New York: New American Library, 1961.

FRANKLIN, JOHN HOPE.   *From Slavery to Freedom: A History of Negro Americans.* 5th ed. New York: Alfred A. Knopf, 1980.

GAY, PETER.   *The Enlightenment: An Interpretation—The Science of Freedom.* New York: W. W. Norton and Company, 1969.

HABERSTAM, DAVID.   *The Fifties.* New York: Villard Books, 1993.

HOFSTADTER, RICHARD.   *The Age of Reform.* New York: Vintage Books, 1955.

———.   *Anti-Intellectualism in American Life.* New York: Vintage Books, 1962.

JOHN, ROBERT W.   "Nineteenth Century Graded Vocal Series." *Journal of Research in Music Education* (Fall 1954): 103–118.

KAMMEN, MICHAEL.   *A Machine That Would Go Of Itself: The Constitution in American Culture.* New York: Vintage Books, 1986.

KAESTLE, CARL F.   *Pillars of the Republic: Common Schools and American Society, 1780–1860.* New York: Hill and Wang, 1983.

KEENE, JAMES A.   *A History of Music Education in the United States.* Hanover, NH: University Press of New England, 1982.

KEGERRIS, RICHARD.   "History of the High School A Cappella Choir." Ph.D. diss., The University of Michigan, 1964.

KLEIBARD, HERBERT M.   *The Forging of the American Curriculum: Essays in Curriculum History and Theory.* New York: Routledge, 1992.

———.   *The Struggle for the American Curriculum: 1893–1958;* reprint, New York: Routledge, Chapman and Hall, 1991.

LABAREE, DAVID F.   *The Making of an American High School: The Credentials Market and the Central High School of Philadelphia, 1838–1939.* New Haven, CT: Yale University Press, 1988.

LEHMANN, NICHOLAS.   *The Promised Land: The Great Black Migration and How it Changed America.* New York: Alfred A. Knopf. 1991.

MARK, MICHAEL L.   *Contemporary Music Education.* 2d ed. New York: Schirmer Books, 1986.

———, and Charles L. Gary. *A History of American Music Education.* New York: Schirmer Books, 1992.

MARSHALL, RAY, AND MARC TUCKER.   *Thinking for a Living: Education and the Wealth of Nations.* New York: Basic Books, 1992.

MAY, ELAINE TYLER.   *Homeward Bound: American Families in the Cold War Era.* New York: Basic Books, 1988.

MAY, HENRY F.   *The Enlightenment in America.* Oxford: Oxford University Press, 1976.

MITCHELL, DOUGLAS E.   "Governance of Schools." In *Encyclopedia of Educational Research,* 6th ed., ed. Marvin C. Alkin. New York: Macmillan Publishing Company,

1992.

OSHINSKY, DAVID M.   *A Conspiracy So Immense: The World of Joe McCarthy.* New York: The Free Press, 1983.

RUTMAN, DARRETT B.   *Winthrop's Boston.* Chapel Hill: University of North Carolina Press, 1965.

SABLOSKY, IRVING L.   *American Music.* Chicago: University of Chicago Press, 1969.

SCHLERETH, THOMAS J.   *Victorian America: Transformations in Everyday Life,* 1876–1915. New York: Harper Perennial, 1991.

SELLERS, CHARLES.   *The Market Revolution: Jacksonian America, 1815–1846.* New York: Oxford Press, 1990.

SILVERMAN, KENNETH.   *A Cultural History of the American Revolution.* New York: Columbia University Press, 1987.

SMITH, PAGE.   *The Constitution: A Documentary and Narrative History.* New York: Morrow Quill Paperbacks, 1980.

SPRING, JOEL.   *The American School: 1642–1992.* 2d edition. New York: Longman, 1990.

THOMAS, RONALD B.   *MMCP Synthesis: A Structure For Music Education.* Washington, DC: U. S. Office of Education, V-008; 6-1999; reprint, New York: Media Materials, n.d.

TYACK, DAVID, AND ELISABETH HANSOT.   *Managers of Virtue: Public School Leadership in America, 1820–1980.* New York: Basic Books, 1982.

VEROFF, JOSEPH, RICHARD A. KULKA, AND ELIZABETH DOUVAN.   *The Inner American: A Self-Portrait from 1957–1976.* New York: Basic Books, 1981.

WASHINGTON, BOOKER T.   *The Story of My Life;* revised, Naperville, IL, n.d.

WILLIAMS, JUAN, AND OTHERS.   *Eyes on the Prize: America's Civil Rights Years, 1954–1965.* With an introduction by Julian Bond. New York: Viking Penguin, 1987.

ZINN, HOWARD.   *A People's History of the United States.* New York: Harper Colophon, 1980; reprint, New York: Harper Perennial, 1990.

2

Philosophies of Music Education

INTRODUCTION AND OBJECTIVES

Philosophers primarily work with ideas; scientists work with events and things. Philosophic method rests on perceptions and interpretations of data, whereas scientific method uses objective and concrete measurements. Philosophy seems to be concerned with theoretical issues, whereas science appears to focus on practical ones. In spite of these differences, both disciplines are concerned with the what, why, and how of things. Investigators, whether scientists or philosophers, observe, analyze, and classify data to formulate theories that bring them come closer to truth. In fact, philosophy and science are inherently connected in that practical aspects of life often cause people to ask probing questions.

From the earliest years of life, human beings are bombarded with information as they interact with the environment. Some of this information is acquired from personal observations and experiences. Other information comes indirectly, through reading; television, radio, and various other media; and other people. Analyzing and categorizing this data leads to general notions about the environment and how it operates, and these notions constitute a theory or philosophy about life.

Philosophy is not static, however. Ideas are altered by each new experience, and in turn, subsequent experiences or interactions with the environment are different, leading to revised convictions and a new set of questions. This cycle—perceiving, questioning, categorizing, and revising—frequently revolves on a subconscious level; only during periods of disquiet do people *consciously* ask questions. Nevertheless, the process by which we acquire understanding or knowledge is the essence of philosophical behavior.

The philosophies discussed in this chapter resulted from this kind of cyclic, intentional inquiry. Throughout history, educational decisions have reflected theories about the why, what, and how of formal instruction. Similarly, music instruction in schools reflected beliefs about the what, why, and how of music—as an artistic discipline and as it relates to general education. School music's dual nature presents a dilemma, however. Music education must be consistent with characteristics that make it musical, but as part of schooling it must also help to accomplish general educational goals. An adequate music education philosophy, then, synthesizes educational and musical viewpoints.

Why is music so integral a part of human life? How are those without musical understanding different from those who have acquired it? Should music instruction be part of every child's educational experiences, and if so, what should its outcome be? Answers to these and similar questions focus school music, guide instructional decision making, and sustain professional commitment. In short, they constitute a working philosophy of music education.

Chapter 2 will help readers to do the following:

* Explain similarities and differences between *traditional* and *nontraditional* philosophies of education.
* Describe the three primary schools of *music philosophy.*
* Explain how John Dewey's *"an experience"* is similar to, yet different from, everyday experiences.
* Explain the phrase *aesthetic qualities* and give one general and one musical example of these qualities.
* Explain the difference between music as *utilitarian* education and music as *aesthetic* education.
* Describe the relationship between *learning* and *experience.*

PHILOSOPHIES OF EDUCATION

Although this part of the text focuses on philosophical differences, it must begin by noting a point of philosophical agreement: All schools of educational philosophy agree that the primary purpose of formal instruction is to sustain society. Transmitting knowledge from one generation to another perpetuates communal life. The process has not always been structured, organized, systematic, or planned, but its value and utility, indeed, its necessity, have never been questioned. Formalizing education symbolized widespread assent to its importance. The fact that schooling persists after more than 2,000 years demonstrates continued agreement about its value as primary transmitter of knowledge.

Given this consensus on the primary purpose of schooling, what accounts for variation among schools within and across historical periods? The answer is that although it is fairly easy to make general assertions about formal education, difficulties arise when trying to apply those beliefs in real-life situations. Beliefs about education are affected by beliefs about other aspects of life and must be reconciled with those other beliefs in order to determine curriculum, pedagogy, and outcomes. Societies throughout history have encountered this quagmire in attempting to specify educational ways and means. The most fundamental and far-reaching of these general issues are discussed next.

Society and the Individual

Formal education sustains a group by focusing on individuals, but societies do not agree about whether the group or the individual should be of primary concern. In some societies, collective good is secondary: It is thought to be a by-product of individual good. Personal achievements are the primary means by which individuals measure themselves and their contributions to society. In turn, society's progress is attributed to individuals, and the aggregate achievements of individuals is the yardstick by which the society measures its development. This viewpoint is characteristic of education philosophies that may be called *traditional,* conservative, or orthodox.

In other communal groups, collective interests come first. Personal achievements are valued only to the extent they benefit society, and personal identity and self-esteem are largely a function of how one is viewed by others. This perspective, by virtue of its departure from the traditional one, is *nontraditional,* liberal, or unorthodox and characterizes the second group of education philosophies.[1]

Ultimately, these differences in priorities regarding the individual and group reflect differing views of human nature. Traditionalists believe that, regardless of ethnic origin, human beings are physical and spiritual beings. Other expressions of this dual nature—rational and irrational, material and immaterial, corporeal and cerebral, body and soul, conscious and subconscious, matter and mind—make it clear that one term in each pair refers to abstract aspects of human experience whereas the other refers to concrete aspects.

In societies in which spiritual human nature is viewed as sacred, that spiritual nature connects humanity with the Creator and human with human. In fact, the soul or spirit is considered to belong to, and to be a part of, the Creator. Thus, it is the essence of an individual but it is also part of a larger, more important or powerful system (God, the universe, humanity, and so forth) and must function accordingly.

Theorists with such beliefs also perceive the soul or spirit as being the superior part of human nature. Consequently, the body and everything associated with it (senses, feeling, and so forth) are considered imperfect and prone to error. They must be held in check by the spirit, and the fact that *spirit* is also called the *conscience* reinforces moral, ethical, and communal implications of this concept.

Nontraditionalists believe that people are unified rather than bipartite beings. Rather than believing that a single nature is shared across ethnic origins, these theorists maintain that environmental factors determine thought and action. A person's or group's ever-changing surroundings shape that person's or group's nature. In turn, human nature changes along with, and because of, its environment. Nontradionalists, then, offer a more

---

[1] See Adrian M. Dupuis, *Philosophy of Education in Historical Perspective* (Lanham, MD: University of America Press, 1985). The traditional group of philosophies is variously referred to in literature as classical, conservative, essentialist, or authoritarian. It includes specific viewpoints such as Idealism, Thomism and Neo-Thomism, Scholasticism, and Aristolelianism. Specific schools in the nontraditional group include Pragmatism, Realism, Naturalism, and Existentialism and are also known as liberal, progressive, modern, and democratic points of view. Also see W. B. Carnochan, *The Battleground of the Curriculum: Liberal Education and American Experience* (Stanford, CA: Stanford University Press, 1993), 22–38.

individualistic perspective of human relationships because to some extent they free individuals from universal or group characteristics.

The Nature of Truth and Wisdom

Beliefs about truth (abstract, fundamental principles governing the world in its broadest sense) and wisdom (the grasp or understanding of these principles) also influence decisions about education. Both traditional and nontraditional schools value truth and wisdom, but they disagree about their nature.[2] Orthodox theorists maintain that there is a core of truth that exists with or without human knowledge of it. This truth is perfect, permanent, and abstract. But truth cannot always be experienced directly or substantiated scientifically because experience and science rely heavily on sensory perceptions that vary as the environment varies. For this reason, sensory information may *assist* humanity in pursuing truth, but only reasoning and logic *reveal* truth and ultimately lead to wisdom. Traditionalists, then, favor developing the intellect (the more abstract or spiritual human attribute) because, as it is strengthened, wisdom—one's understanding of truth—increases.

Traditionalists believe that because truth exists and is knowable it can be taught by those who know and understand it. People who know and understand come closer to perfection than the rest of society and serve as role models by virtue of their wisdom. From this perspective, teaching or sharing truth is the most important contribution that individuals can make to a group.

In contrast, nontraditionalists believe truth is a method or paradigm—a way of knowing and understanding—so that human knowledge at any given time is the only existing truth. Truth is primarily a product of experience and is ever-changing, imperfect, and incomplete, like the sensory information from which it emerges. Truth's inchoate nature is a positive characteristic, however, because it generates human curiosity. By extension, curiosity, which exemplifies the desire to know and understand, represents inherently human potential. Everyone has aptitude for knowing, although the extent to which people *desire* to know and are driven by this desire varies. Nontraditionalists believe that the desire to know is wisdom. The wisest people are those who recognize the insufficiency of human knowledge and constantly seek to expand knowledge. Thus, though these people may teach processes and may share what they have learned, they cannot teach or share truth because they, too, are seeking it.

Clearly, these beliefs about truth, wisdom, and human nature influence choices about educational method and content, as do many other broad issues (ethics and morality, for example). Although the scope of this text precludes discussing all of these, one additional issue—quality of life—is discussed next because it is particularly relevant to music education. Theories about music provide information that will be pertinent to that discussion.

[2] Ibid.

PHILOSOPHIES OF MUSIC

When Alexander Baumgarten first used the term *aesthetics* for what he described as the science of perception (knowledge acquired through the senses), he was naming a relatively new but increasingly accepted direction in art theory. By and large, previous art theories had focused on the more concrete and objective aspects of artworks, so that art and music were described in ethical, mathematical, and even scientific terms. During the latter part of the seventeenth century, however, traditional ways of describing art began to give way to theories defining art as a form of human expression. Descriptions of art now focused on factors related to the artist or the perceiver of artworks. By validating perception as a way of knowing, Baumgarten accelerated the shift from objective to subjective concerns. Some years later, largely as a result of the work of Immanuel Kant, the term *aesthetic* began to assume its contemporary meaning.[3]

In the twentieth century the term *aesthetic* refers to objective characteristics of art (form and structure, sound frequencies, instrumentation, brush strokes, tints, colors) and also encompasses a host of subjective characteristics (beauty, taste, feeling, value, and expression) that stem from the nineteenth-century concern with how people perceive and react to art, and why. For this reason, all of the philosophies of music discussed here are *aesthetic* philosophies because they are views of music as an art form and as it is perceived. Generally, these theories focus on four issues: (1) what music is and what it means, (2) how music communicates this meaning, (3) how musical elements affect perception and meaning, and (4) why music arouses human feeling. (See Table 2–1.)

All of the perspectives discussed here can be traced to Greece, where music was shrouded in mystery, as were other aspects of human life.[4] Greek theorists ascribed music's origin and power to gods in much the same way that they attributed other inexplicable events to divinities. But considering music, dance, and poetry as a single art form helped to make music less mysterious. Poetry contributed to music's rhythmic nature and gave musical sounds more or less concrete meanings. Moreover, textual meaning was more powerful when combined with music. Consequently, music was valued as a medium through which many kinds of meaning were transmitted. Some time later, music's association with numerical principles led theorists to value it as a source of wisdom, one which offered insight about the essence of nature and the universe. All of these are *heteronomist* viewpoints, because heteronomists see the meaning conveyed through music as different in nature from musical sound.[5] Music's meaning is extramusical because it results from appending something to musical sound, and it is nonmusical because it is primarily con-

---

[3] See Ted Cohen and Paul Guyer, "Introduction to Kant's Aesthetics: from *Essays in Kant's Aesthetics,*" in *Aesthetics: A Critical Anthology,* George Dickie, Richard Scalafan, and Ronald Robin, eds. (New York: St Martin's Press, 1989), 306–314. Because Kant claimed that Baumgarten's subjective use of the term *aesthetic* deviated from its original Greek meaning, he sought to restore some measure of objectivity to it by focusing on the conditions of perception rather than solely on the act of perceiving.

[4] See Edward Lippman, *A History of Muscial Aesthetics* (Lincoln, NE: University of Nebraska Press, 1992).

[5] See Eduard Hanslick, *The Beautiful in Music,* trans. with an introduction by Morris Weitz (Indianapolis, IN: Bobbs-Merrill Company, 1957).

TABLE 2–1   Music Philosophies

Heteronomists		Autonomists	Formal/Absolute Expressionists
Referentialists	Expressionists	Formalists or Absolutists	
Meaning is *extrinsic* to musical sound.	Meaning is *extrinsic* to musical sound.	Meaning is *intrinsic* to musical sound.	Meaning is *intrinsic* to musical sound.
Musical meaning is *denotative.**	Musical meaning is *denotative.*	Musical meaning is *denotative.*	Musical meaning is *denotative* and *connotative.*
Musical sound refers to nonmusical things.	Musical sound refers to specific emotional states.	Musical sound refers to itself.	Musical sound refers to itself but suggests or resembles qualities of nature and emotive states.
Musical sound imitates or expresses • specific emotions (joy, sorrow, etc.) • people, objects, ideas		Musical sound expresses or conveys • unilateral interactions between its essential qualities (pitch level, density, volume, etc., of individual sounds and instruments) • multilateral interactions among its essential qualities (intervals, scales, chords, musical forms, instrument groupings, etc.)	Musical sound expresses • unilateral interactions between its essential qualities (pitch level, density, volume, etc., of individual sounds and instruments) • multilateral interactions among its essential qualities (intervals, scales, chords, musical forms, instrument groupings, etc.)

*Denotative = representational or referential.

veyed through something other than musical sound. Nonmusical meaning results then, when musical sound is said to represent a person, place, thing or idea.

Heteronomists can be divided into two smaller groups: *referentialists,* who believe that music's meaning is derived from its references to or imitations of nonmusical things, and 2) *expressionists,* who maintain that music has meaning because it expresses the emotions of the composer, the text, and/or the performer. The expressionist viewpoint is in the same vein as the Greek ascription of emotional states to musical forms and tuning systems, which were believed to evoke specific reactions in listeners. Similarly, the "doctrine of affections" that was so important in Baroque music reflects referential and expressionist ideas.

The second primary philosophical view of music, the *autonomist* school, became prominent in eighteenth-century Germany and is diametrically opposed to heteronomist beliefs although it, too, has roots in Greece.[6] Grecian poet/musicians adhered to musical forms and tunings because, among other things, they believed that these forms *were* the

[6] Ibid. Also see Carl Dalhaus, *The Idea of Absolute Music,* trans. Roger Lustig (Chicago, IL: University of Chicago Press, 1989).

meaning of music. Likewise, eighteenth-century autonomists (also known as formalists or absolutists) maintained that meaning conveyed through music resulted from the organization of musical sounds—the various forms of music and its internal structure. They believed that the meaning one derives from music is purely musical or intrinsic, a function of the actual musical sounds and their interactions. Consequently, autonomists also assert that music has no inherent relationship to nonmusical things or emotional states and that any such meaning attached to music is artificial. The autonomist position is most often applied to instrumental music: If there is text, musical sound is thought to be related to it; by contrast, instrumental music has no text and conveys meaning and affects emotion through sound itself.

Formal expressionism or *absolute expressionism,* the third school of thought about music, strikes a balance between the first two theories, combining aspects of each. It is autonomistic in holding that musical meaning results in part from musical form and structure. At the same time it asserts that formal aspects of music do in fact express something, which is the heteronomist position. However, formal or absolute expressionists are *not* referentialists because they do not believe that music imitates or refers to specific nonmusical things. Rather, they propose that musical sound has characteristics that are similar to those of emotions.[7] Stated another way, music has intrinsic qualities that make it expressive. Thus, its imitation of or reference to things outside of itself are not vital, but are optional.

Exactly what do the formal characteristics of music express? Unlike the ancient Greeks and Baroque theorists, formal expressionists do not believe that music conveys *specific* emotions. They do believe, however, that musical forms express a rhythmic quality, a dynamism that is common to life experiences and to emotion or feeling. Experiences and feeling constantly move or change, often almost imperceptibly, and although musical sound does not *imitate* them, it bears a *likeness* to them. Qualities of musical sound (pitch, volume, timbre, duration) and the organization of musical sound (sonata form, fugues, symphonies, and so forth) generate responses in listeners that are akin to those generated by life and feeling.[8]

PHILOSOPHIES OF MUSIC EDUCATION

Music's prominent role in human life does not of itself justify a place in school programs. In fact, it would seem to suggest that formal education in music is unnecessary. Why, then, do societies decide to include music in formal education? The answer to this question amounts to each society's philosophy of music education. Earlier in this chapter, the authors pointed out that music education philosophy is a hybrid entity, combining beliefs about music and education. Now that each of these components has been examined separately, various ways of combining them can be presented.

---

[7] See Susanne K. Langer, *Philosophy in a New Key,* 3rd ed. (Cambridge, MA: Harvard University Press, 1957); and Bennett Reimer, *A Philosophy of Music Education,* 2d ed. (Englewood Cliffs, NJ: Prentice Hall, 1989).

[8] Ibid.

Utilitarian and Aesthetic Philosophies

Opinions about music education's contribution to society reflect one of two perspectives: utilitarian and aesthetic.[9] The *utilitarian* perspective explains the value of music study in terms used to validate other subject areas. The utilitarian position is that music education helps to develop qualities such as self-discipline and cooperative spirit. Furthermore, students involved in school music programs demonstrate higher levels of academic achievement, better self-images, deeper senses of self-worth, and better reading skills. In addition, music affords opportunities for students to explore and develop their innate capacity for creative self-expression.

The aesthetic viewpoint claims that music education *may* lead to such nonmusical outcomes, but its primary value is its ability to heighten or strengthen students' sensitivity. Musical instruction may ultimately improve the quality of students' lives even after they have left the educational environment.

Both points of view have merit, and music instruction in American schools has always reflected one or the other of them. The utilitarian rationale is credited with helping Lowell Mason and others win music's initial place in education programs. Present-day music educators continue to offer this rationale for what they do because it is easy to articulate and is clearly understood by those who decide the fate of music in schools. But it is difficult to maintain music's place solely on a utilitarian basis because such outcomes are generic; they apply to most areas of study and do not focus on the unique contribution of any single discipline. What is more, other school subjects are better suited than music to accomplish utilitarian goals. A more critical problem, however, is that the utilitarian rationale focuses on nonmusical outcomes of music classes rather than emphasizing the intrinsic worth of music subject matter. On the other hand, the aesthetic rationale for music education focuses on music's unique contribution to educational goals. It asserts that music merits study because of what it is and what that essence does for children.

During the 1930s, American philosopher John Dewey (1859–1952) added another dimension to debates about music in formal education. Although Dewey conceived and initially presented his concept to shed light on ordinary experiences, his "*an* experience" is known today as the aesthetic experience.[10] Dewey aimed to show that aesthetic experiences are merely enrichments of average experiences. The ramifications of this notion become clearer as the discussion progresses.

"An Experience" and Music

Experience in its broadest sense is at the heart of Dewey's philosophy. This inescapable consequence of human existence plays a critical role in his views about education. For Dewey, experience is the active process by which people gather information about the environment. They understand and make sense of the world as a result of interacting with it.

---

[9] See Reimer, *A Philosophy of Music Education.*

[10] See John Dewey, *Art As Experience* (New York: G. P. Putnam's Sons, 1934; reprint, New York: Perigee Books, 1980).

Whereas traditional theories focus on how the environment affects humanity, Dewey argues that each person plays an important role in shaping his or her own experiences or environment. In this way the quality of people's experiences is largely a matter of their own actions. In addition, when people have positive unforgettable experiences, it is often as much because of something they have done as it is because of something that was done to them. Because these extraordinary experiences are special instances of ordinary ones, they are best understood by comparing them with their average counterparts.

First, special experiences, like ordinary ones, are active, interactive, and reciprocal, an exchange between the person and the environment; each acts on the other. However, this interaction is more balanced, or equal, during special experiences than during ordinary ones.

Second, all experiences move in stages, but special ones are more cohesive and continuous. Whereas ordinary experiences involve start-and-stop sequences, "*an* experience" is marked by seamlessness. It is unified to the point that one remembers it as a whole rather than in parts. Recalled intact and complete, it becomes greater than the sum of its parts.

The third distinction between ordinary and special experiences is closely related to the second. Whereas average experiences often end prematurely for a number of reasons, special ones are self-propelled and demand to be followed through. Moreover, the end of these experiences is more a consummation than a cessation, coming as the natural completion of movement or energy inherent in the experience.

Special experiences also differ from everyday ones in having a distinctive unity. According to Dewey, most ordinary experiences involve some degree of emotion, although the experiences are either primarily intellectual (seeing a relationship between action and consequence) or primarily practical (connecting a means to an end).[11] By contrast, *an* experience occurs when feeling melds with the practical and the intellectual in such a way that neither of these dominates. Because of this fusion, the special experience is self-serving and fulfilling. It is worthwhile and meaningful because of what it is and not because of what it taught, what it accomplished, or how it felt. Special experiences are their own means and ends.

Finally, these experiences are unified in that each stage brings together all that preceded it, and this ongoing synthesis informs the stages that follow. This explains why each phase naturally and logically leads into the next. The experience is continually reconstructed so that all of its elements fit. Everything that takes place needs to take place, in light of the overall experience.

A similar assimilation and reconstruction happen on a more general level. The very occurrence of such an experience implies a readiness for it: Experiences prior to it have prepared the person for what is about to occur. Moreover, the person is not the same after this experience. All subsequent experiences are colored by this one, and in this way, the interaction reconstructs the person's life. *An* experience, as the exception rather than the rule, occurs at unexpected times, but once achieved, it is a constant reminder of the po-

---

[11] Dewey uses the word *emotion* to mean a general feeling, something more akin to interest or involvement than to specific emotions such as happiness or sadness. This interest or involvement is "the moving and cementing force" that unifies various parts of the experience.

tential in *all* experience. Dewey contends that the special experience, by virtue of its self-sufficiency and individualizing quality, stands in marked contrast to other interactions "as an enduring memorial of what [all experience] may be."[12]

Music As Aesthetic Education

Taken together, the general philosophies of education, philosophies of music and music education, and Dewey's concept of the special experience presented here help music educators formulate a working philosophy of music education. The synthesizing begins by acknowledging that there are two sides—objective and subjective—to human life.[13] The *objective* side of life is practical, instrumental. It encompasses actions necessary for survival and for maintaining equilibrium in an ever-changing environment. Eating, sleeping, drinking, and breathing are examples of objective human behaviors. All of these actions have a rhythmic or fluctuating quality. In addition, they move people from one physical state to another—from imbalance to balance, from tension to relaxation, and so forth. Eating, for example, leads one from a state of hunger to one of fulfillment, and the act of eating—the process of moving from hunger to satiation—is marked by subtle, even imperceptible stages or progressions. Similarly, sleeping moves one from fatigue to restedness and through the various states in between. This movement or rhythm resembles the rhythm of nature: Fall changes to winter, day evolves into night, the sun rises and sets. Such rhythmic movement is very much a part of human existence.

Objective actions may generate feelings, which account for the subjective side of human existence. As objective behaviors help people maintain balance with their surroundings, these behaviors also affect them in myriad personal ways that cannot be seen or articulated precisely. This subjectivity has the potential for increasing the value, enjoyment, benefit, or meaning of the objective action that generates it, and when such enhancement occurs, the quality of ordinary, routine existence improves.

A simple illustration: Eating fulfills its objective function when it relieves hunger, but eating an especially tasty meal goes beyond satisfying a basic human need. By meeting the need for nourishment in a manner exceeding what is required or expected, this tasty meal leads to a deeper sense of fulfillment and remains in memory as a reminder that eating and nourishment can have an added dimension. This specific act of eating is an enriched one, and the quality of existence at the time of the meal is elevated.

Parallels can be drawn between life experience and musical experience. First, music making can be likened to objective needs that are basic to human survival. The ability to make music is one of the skills that sets humanity apart from other animal species. Making music satisfies the human impulse for creative self-expression—the desire to symbolize experiences. The manner in which the elements of music (melody, rhythm, harmony, texture, form, expressive qualities) are used reflects the movement or rhythm and feeling inherent in all human experiences. (For example, melodies generate tension by ascending

---

[12] Ibid., 36.

[13] See Langer, *Philosophy in a New Key;* and Susanne K. Langer, *Feeling and Form* (New York: Charles Scribner's Sons, 1953).

and relieve this tension when they descend. Dominant-seventh chords create tension that is resolved by tonic chords. Anticipation generated during a development section is relieved by recapitulation.) When teachers refine students' ability to perceive the elements of music as they interact to simulate this ebb and flow, they help students recognize, explore, understand, appreciate, and become more attuned to the aspects of rhythm and feeling in human life.

Once students are attuned to this rhythmic or emotive side of life, their chances of undergoing enriched experiences increase. (Recall that the *potential* for unforgettable experience is found in most ordinary ones.) Having had enriched experiences, students will seek them because they are fulfilling in a way that ordinary experiences are not. Think about the eating analogy again. The tasty meal provides deeper satisfaction or fulfillment than more routine meals. Moreover, the tasty meal suggests that most meals have the *potential* for exceeding their objective function. Thus, given a choice, one is more likely to seek this kind of enriched eating experience again. The quality of a person's future existence is altered in that he or she will no doubt *consciously* seek to make it more fulfilling.

This notion of enriched experience relates to music in that a composer's resolution of musical problems sometimes goes beyond what is required, just as the resolution of basic needs occasionally exceeds routine demands. Indeed, the relative greatness of musical compositions is largely determined by the extent to which composers meet and surpass our expectations.[14]

In a very real way, then, musical works symbolize life experiences. They present human existence in concentrated, miniature form, and through them people relive and reexperience the best or most fulfilling aspects of existence. Using the earlier criterion for greatness, the greater the musical work, the deeper its effect and meaning. This is because great works generate emotive responses similar to those that accompany special life experiences, allowing listeners, performers, and composers to reexperience them in pure, abstract form. Through carefully structured educational interactions with music, teachers heighten students' sensitivity to the musical qualities that convey feeling. By doing so they also enable students to recognize and respond to greatness or richness in music and, by extension, in life.

Music's educational value is significant, although its contribution differs from that of science or mathematics. The more students are able to discern in music and the more they understand music, the greater their appreciation for music and the potential it symbolizes. Furthermore, because their ability to interact with and respond to the expressive elements of music is heightened, their musical experiences enrich their lives.

Ideally, comprehensive education develops the mind, the body, and the spirit. The study of music is especially related to the last of these objectives. This is what "music as aesthetic education" is all about. Given the subjective nature of musical responses, students should not be taught *what* or *how* to feel, but their *ability* to feel will develop if they are allowed to experience emotion-packed and meaningful events in miniature through musical compositions.

---

[14] See Leonard B. Meyer, *Emotion and Meaning in Music* (Chicago, IL: University of Chicago Press, 1956) for in-depth discussion of relationships between expectation and responses to music.

Undoubtedly, this chapter raises as many questions as it answers. How, for instance, do these ideas serve as a guide for actual music instruction? What kinds of experiences should music teachers provide to heighten students' responsiveness to aesthetic qualities in music? In other arts? In life generally? What difference does it make whether music is taught for utilitarian or aesthetic purposes?

The next part of the text gives answers to these questions. For now, it is sufficient to note that almost any educational decision music teachers make, no matter how slight or seemingly unimportant, implies a philosophical point of view. This fact alone makes philosophy worth thinking about. Before reading further, consider how a music educator might go about justifying music education for the local school board, the parents of the child who lives next door, or readers of the local newspaper. What does music education offer that is important enough to merit its place in school curricula? Write brief notes and place them in the back of the text. After completing the text, review these notes and see if they still reflect your philosophical views.

STUDY AND DISCUSSION QUESTIONS

1. Is music a universal language? Justify your answer.
2. How does the use of musical elements in popular music differ from their use in classical music? How is the use similar? Do these similarities and differences affect the way people respond to each kind of music? Explain your answer.
3. Select any one of your favorite instrumental compositions, classical or popular. Try to explain what you like about it in musical terms. Does this description express how you really feel about this selection? If your response to this last question is yes, what does that tell you about your response to the composition? If your answer is no, does any information in this chapter account for your inability to articulate your feelings about the composition? Speculate aloud.
4. Does music appreciation increase as musical knowledge and understanding increase? Explain your answer citing specific examples as necessary.
5. Choose a short instrumental composition. Prepare a five- to ten-minute script that presents this selection to a friend or to your classmates in one of the following ways: (a) from a referentialist perspective, (b) from a formalist perspective, (c) from an expressionist perspective, or (d) from an absolute expressionist perspective.
    Now, respond to the following:
    a. Do you think your audience gained the understanding you were trying to convey? Why, or why not?
    b. Would you have had better success using one of the other approaches? If you think so, tell which one and explain your answer.

REFERENCES AND RECOMMENDED SOURCES

ADLER, MORTIMER J.   *Art, the Arts, and the Great Ideas.* New York: Macmillan Publishing Co., 1994.

BARROW, ROBIN, AND RONALD WOODS.   *An Introduction to Philosophy of Education.* 3rd ed. New York: Routledge, 1988.

CARNOCHAN, W. B.   *The Battleground of the Curriculum: Liberal Education and American Experience.* Stanford, CA: Stanford University Press, 1993.

COHEN, TED, AND PAUL GUYER.   "Introduction to Kant's Aesthetics: from *Essays in Kant's Aesthetics.*" In *Aesthetics: A Critical Anthology,* ed. George Dickie, Richard Scalafan, and Ronald Roblin, 306–314. New York: St, Martin's Press, 1989.

COOKE, DERYCK.   *The Language of Music.* Oxford: Oxford University Press, 1959.

DALHAUS, CARL.   *Esthetics of Music.* Trans. William Austin; reprint, Cambridge, MA: Cambridge University Press, 1988.

————.   *The Idea of Absolute Music.* Trans. Roger Lustig. Chicago, IL: University of Chicago Press, 1989.

DEWEY, JOHN.   *Art As Experience.* New York: G. P. Putnam's Sons, 1934; reprint, New York: Perigee Books, 1980.

DUPUIS, ADRIAN M.   *Philosophy of Education in Historical Perspective.* Lanham, MD: University Press of America, 1985.

EATON, MARCIA MUELDER.   *Basic Issues in Aesthetics.* Belmont, CA: Wadsworth Publishing Company, 1988.

HANSLICK, EDUARD.   *The Beautiful in Music.* Trans. Gustav Cohen. Ed. with an introduction by Morris Weitz. Indianapolis, IN: Bobbs-Merrill Company, 1957.

LANGER, SUSANNE K.   *Feeling and Form.* New York: Charles Scribner's Sons, 1953.

————.   *Philosophy in a New Key.* 3rd ed. Cambridge: Harvard University Press, 1957.

MEYER, LEONARD B.   *Emotion and Meaning in Music.* Chicago, IL: University of Chicago Press, 1956.

LIPPMAN, EDWARD.   *A History of Musical Aesthetics.* Lincoln, NE: University of Nebraska Press, 1992.

REIMER, BENNETT.   *A Philosophy of Music Education.* 2d ed. Englewood Cliffs, NJ: Prentice Hall, 1989.

Part II

Music Education: Philosophy in Action

This part of the text is primarily about educational psychology: human growth and development in educational settings. Whereas Part I examined events in music education history and discussed theoretical and philosophical beliefs underlying those events, the following chapters focus on practical aspects of formal music instruction. Chapters 3, 4, and 5 discuss what should be studied in music classes and examine ways in which this material can be organized to realize the potential of music instruction. Because realizing this potential ultimately rests on teaching and learning, both of these are examined. Learning is discussed before teaching because effective instructors take the ways people learn into account and attempt to create environments most conducive to learning. Before proceeding, however, another issue requires attention.

The saying "You live and learn" has a good deal of truth to it. People learn constantly—intentionally, incidentally, or accidently, whether they want to or not, inside or outside of school. As this is the case, the perpetuation of formal schooling implies that school experiences are intended to impart information or skills that life experiences do not, or that they are meant to impart them in a different way. For this reason, teachers must know exactly what schools are intended to do. They must understand differences in teaching and learning that occur inside schools rather than outside. The remainder of this introduction is devoted to clarifying these differences.[1]

To begin, consider the following statements, paying special attention to words in italics:

He *taught* me a *lesson* I'll never forget.
Well, that'll *teach* them.
That's the end of today's *lesson*.

[1] The importance of these differences is driven home in a similar discussion in G. David Peters and Robert F. Miller, *Music Teaching and Learning* (New York: Longman, Inc., 1982), 4–7.

You'll *know* better next time.
I hope they've *learned* their *lesson*.
Tomorrow, I'll *teach* you about steam engines.

Given the context in which these statements are usually made, it is fairly certain that only the third and last statements refer to formal instruction. But read all of these statements again and try to imagine each one in the opposite context. Imagine, for instance, that the first statement is made by a student in reference to a good schoolteacher or that the second one is said by an exhilarated band director following a rehearsal. The contexts are interchangeable because no matter where teaching and learning occur, the processes and the outcomes involved are the same: In the situation referred to in each statement, someone experiences or undergoes something that is intended to make them different in some way.

Similarities notwithstanding, instances of teaching and learning outside of school ought to differ from instances in school. For the moment, think of the term *education* as describing teaching and learning that take place outside of schools, and think of *schooling* as referring to teaching and learning that occur in schools. With this distinction in mind, study the following illustrations. Then try to determine which one is "schooling" in this more restricted sense.

ILLUSTRATION 1

After school, Johnny walks into the house and shouts, "I ain't gonna play with Tommy no more." His sister replies, "You mean 'I'm NOT gonna play with Tommy ANYmore.'" Johnny echoes in a somewhat quieter voice, "I'm NOT gonna play with Tommy ANYmore" and then proceeds to tell why at the top of his voice.

An hour or so later, Johnny storms into the kitchen, throws his catcher's mitt on the table, and says, "I ain't playin' with *them* no more." His father looks up from the soup he's stirring and says, "You mean 'I'm NOT playing with them ANYmore.'" Tommy echoes: "I'm NOT playing with them ANYmore" and stomps upstairs to his room.

After dinner, when his sister refuses to get off the phone so that he can call his friend, Tommy exclaims, "I ain't takin' messages for you no more!" His mother calls out from the other room, "You mean 'I'm NOT taking messages for you ANYmore.'" Tommy leaves the house, slamming the door behind him and echoing his mother under his breath.

ILLUSTRATION 2

Pamela raises her hand in frustration. She's tried the same experiment three times and it hasn't turned out correctly. She's followed all of the directions, so she can't imagine what the problem is.

Dr. Marcus walks over and asks how she can help. Pamela briefly explains the situation, and Dr. Marcus asks Pamela to do the experiment again while she watches. Dr. Marcus also asks Pamela to tell her everything she's going to do before she does it and to explain why she's doing it. Pamela sighs and begins the experiment. After she explains the fourth step, Dr. Marcus stops her and asks questions about the explanation. Before long, Pamela exclaims, "Oh, yeah!" and restates the fourth step correctly along with its rationale. Dr. Marcus confirms the explanation, then leaves Pamela to complete the experiment alone.

At the end of class, as Pamela prepares to leave the lab, Dr. Marcus asks if the experiment worked the last time. Pamela nods and smiles. Dr. Marcus then asks Pamela if she knows why the experiment didn't work the first three times. Pamela nods more vigorously before explaining the mistakes she had been making in the fourth step.

The teaching used in both illustrations aims to alter a specific behavior, but notice that one learner knows the reason for the teacher's responses or suggestions whereas the other learner does not. This instructional difference affects the quality of the learning. In Illustration 1, Tommy's family reacts to his grammar by offering correct statements for him to imitate. One can assume that on some level, Tommy understands he is having to repeat statements because something was wrong with them. Even so, he does not know precisely what is wrong or how to correct the error on his own. In addition, he does not know why it matters whether he says one or the other of these versions.

Now consider Illustration 2. The need for behavioral change is more obvious in this case because Pamela has tried to complete the experiment three times without success. She knows that something is wrong, although she does not know just what it is. She wants help. What is more, Pamela comes away from her experience knowing what she did wrong and how to avoid making the same error in the future.

Another thing to note is that in the second illustration, the student is involved in the teaching as well as in the learning. This is a second important difference between the two teaching *procedures.* The teaching in the first illustration is done through modeling: Tommy heard the three models, noticed that they differed from his statements, and immediately imitated them. On the other hand, Dr. Marcus's procedure actually allowed Pamela to teach herself. Pamela apparently had the information needed to resolve her problem; Dr. Marcus simply assisted her with recalling it so that she could apply it to the situation at hand. If necessary, Pamela can now tell someone what she was doing wrong. Moreover, she can probably spot this error in subsequent assignments (or in the work of a classmate) and correct it without Dr. Marcus's help. Tommy seems unable to exercise this kind of self-correction, and herein lies an obvious difference between *outcomes,* or quality of learning.

Illustration 1 is an example of education in the restricted sense previously discussed, whereas Illustration 2 demonstrates schooling—not because of the context in which these incidents occurred but because of the teaching procedure and outcome in each instance. In the "education" example, teaching is reactive, opportunistic, and corrective: The teacher waits until the need for teaching (or learning) presents itself. In addition, the effectiveness of this teaching—its outcomes in terms of learning—depends on the teacher's presence. After two "lessons" Tommy does not use correct grammar without a model, a teacher to follow. One can imagine that scenes such as that in Illustration I would have to be enacted many times before the teaching achieves the desired long-range effect. Tommy's learning experiences have not made him independent of his instructors.

In the "schooling" example, the teaching appears to be opportunistic, reactive, and corrective, but on closer examination it becomes clear that this is not the case. For one thing, Dr. Marcus gave Pamela the information she required to complete the assignment before it was actually needed. Stated another way, Dr. Marcus had planned that the experiment come after the lesson that prepared it. This mode of teaching allowed Pamela to take an active role in the present learning experience. Perhaps more important, Dr. Marcus's teaching procedures enables Pamela to correct her own mistakes in similar experiences that may occur later. Pamela has become independent of her instructor in that she knows what her error was, she can recognize it, and she can now correct herself. She is more likely to remember her mistake and how it was resolved because of the manner in which she "discovered" it. Because Pamela has information that will help her avoid making the same mistake again, the teaching here is preventive. Moreover, once it appeared that Pamela had learned, Dr. Marcus went one step further to reinforce the new behavior.

Differences between education and schooling as discussed here are critical because of the kind of teaching they involve and the quality of learning they generate. These differences are summarized as follows:

Education is	Schooling is
corrective	preventive
opportunistic	a priori (before the fact)
random/haphazard	systematic/organized
passive	active
Education promotes	Schooling promotes
learner dependence	learner independence
short-term behavior change	long-term behavior change (memory)

Distinctions between education and schooling have been made primarily for clarification and definition. Schools will never be free of "education," nor should they be. Students will always influence each other and learn from their mistakes and interactions with other students. Moreover, "education" does not only occur outside of schools, nor does "schooling" always occur inside. The craft class offered at a neighborhood recreation center after school may be a better example of schooling than the fourth-grade math class at the local elementary school. Similarly, the Little League baseball team's practice sessions might well be better examples of schooling than the high school's Dramatics Club rehearsals. It might also be that the "school of hard knocks" applies as much to what goes on in the middle school English class as it does to daily life experiences. The procedures and the outcomes of teaching make the difference, not the context or setting.

The following chapters about curriculum, learning, and teaching describe what is supposed to happen in schools. Concepts discussed in this introduction are revisited and elaborated on to point out what teachers should be doing each day in the classroom. Teachers who want to ensure that quality learning takes place will want to use procedures that are most likely to generate it.

Having completed this introduction, readers should note that the full quotation partially presented at the beginning reads: "We live and learn, but never the wiser grow."

3

Curriculum:
A Model
for Music Instruction

INTRODUCTION AND OBJECTIVES

Curriculum is defined in three ways. For some educators, it is what students must do as part of schooling. This definition reflects the term's original Latin meaning[1] and emphasizes skill development. From this perspective, the ability to do a thing indicates that one possesses some degree of theoretical knowledge. For other educators, the term *curriculum* refers to what students must know as a result of schooling. This definition emphasizes subject matter and suggests that skills and theoretical knowledge are acquired simultaneously or that skill is less important than knowledge. A third definition refers to specific instructional methods or philosophies such as those developed by Carl Orff, Zoltán Kodály, Shinichi Suzuki, Edwin Gordon, and others. These methods typically specify skills to be developed, theoretical knowledge to be acquired, and the order in which both should be presented, thus implying that skills and knowledge are equally important educational concerns.

The definition used in this text is closest to the third one. As used here, *curriculum* is a broad sequence of music courses providing comprehensive information about music and facilitating development of music skills in order to promote musical understanding. The terms *broad* and *comprehensive* refer to the quantity and breadth of courses. *Sequence* refers to hierarchies of subject matter and skill development.

In addition to encompassing doing and knowing, this definition underscores several aspects of school programs that the other two definitions only suggest. First, notice that outcomes conveyed in the working definition are general and are equally appropriate for

---

[1] *Curriculum* is a diminutive of *course* (as in something to run through, or a runway), derived from the Latin *currus* (meaning racecourse). The Latin term is, no doubt, associated with the athletic games in which entrants ran specific courses or races and in which games took place within a set time frame and circuit (derived from the Latin *circus,* meaning circular or oval-shaped).

all students regardless of instructional level. This aspect acknowledges that, although there is a time and place in school programs for specialized knowledge and skills, the most successful schooling first seeks to provide basic knowledge and achieve general goals that benefit and apply to everyone. In the same way, most college programs are primarily general music programs. Many music courses required for specific degrees or music specializations are also required for music degrees generally, because there is a body of knowledge and skills that all musicians must acquire.

A second aspect of this working definition of curriculum is that, in keeping with the concerns of this text, the subject matter is specifically music, as evidenced by the content (i.e., music courses), skills (music skills), and knowledge (music understanding).

Chapter 3 will enable readers to do the following:

- Define the term *music curriculum.*
- List and describe at least four commonly used ways of organizing school
  music curricula.
- Explain the phrase *spiral curriculum.*
- Describe an ideal school music curriculum.

CURRICULUM AND GENERAL EDUCATION PHILOSOPHY

Considering that it is virtually impossible to make educational decisions without implying a philosophical position, it is not surprising that school programs reflect each of the education philosophies discussed in Chapter 2.

For example, the traditional belief that human beings are rational creatures underlies educational programs that aim to develop the intellect through a traditional or basic curriculum. Accordingly, only academic subjects involving intellectual and rational tasks merit the label *schooling.* Subjects involving the senses and the body are considered extracurricular, if included at all. This academic curriculum is also authoritarian and teacher-centered, in keeping with traditional notions about the nature of wisdom and truth.

Compare the traditional school program with the curricular recommendations of more nontraditional education philosophers, who maintain that schooling should emphasize ethical concerns. Because children are basically and naturally good, they reason, it follows that children's needs, wants, and interests are good or morally neutral rather than evil. These needs, wants, and interests are, in fact, entirely natural and only require proper direction and development. In addition, these philosophers reject the mind/body dichotomy in favor of educating the whole child. Thus, they believe that school programs should extend beyond academic subjects to include music, art, physical education, and the like. In short, curriculum includes everything that takes place under the direction or control of the school. School programs should also be child- and problem-centered, practical, and close to real-life experience, and program content should be determined at least in part by the students' interests.

When developing instructional programs, each philosophical group evaluates school subjects according to the group's educational objectives. Each group's curriculum recommendations will include subjects that go farthest toward realizing that group's desired educational outcomes, and other subjects, though worthwhile, will receive less attention or be excluded altogether because they contribute less to achieving these objectives. Thus, this philosophy-based decision-making process establishes curricular priorities and ultimately determines music education's status in the curriculum. Regardless of the status given to music programs in schools, there are usually three features that these programs share. The next section of the chapter discusses these features.

SHARED ASPECTS OF MUSIC CURRICULUM

The Hidden Curriculum

In addition to the organized programs to be discussed, there is a hidden curriculum at work in every school that is so pervasive it usually goes unnoticed by students and staff. This aspect of schooling encompasses all school experiences not explicitly included in the official education program. "Thus, to the extent that school rules and regulations or the physical or social environment influences what students learn [and why and how they learn], they are part of the 'hidden curriculum.'"[2]

Learning to cope with delay, idleness, interruption, criticism, regimentation, peer pressure, and rejection are just a few of a school's unofficial or "hidden" offerings, and this curriculum is learned in much the same way the official curriculum content is learned. Furthermore, some educators contend that many aspects of this hidden curriculum may have nearly as much bearing on success or failure in school as academic achievement does.

Willing or not, all teachers play as critical a role in teaching the hidden curriculum and developing its skills as they do in conveying the content of their disciplines. Educators are teaching—indirectly or directly, by word or by deed—every moment of the time they spend with students.

The Spiral Curriculum

A number of the programs described in the following sections are based to some extent on a spiral concept. The term *spiral curriculum* refers to vertical or sequential aspects of the curriculum. Jerome Bruner, a participant in the Woods Hole Conference, was among the first of recent educational psychologists to propose a cyclic approach to curriculum development, and curriculum planners quickly adopted this idea for use in a variety of disciplines, including music.

Bruner suggests that "any idea [concept] can be represented honestly and usefully in the thought forms of children of school age."[3] These concepts or bits of information are

---

[2] Louis Fischer, "The Constitution and the Curriculum," in *Curriculum Handbook: Administration and Theory,* ed. by Louis Rubin (Boston: Allyn and Bacon, Inc., 1977), 253.

[3] Jerome Bruner, *The Process of Education* (Cambridge: Harvard University Press, 1960; reprint, Cambridge: Harvard University Press, 1977), 33.

not focused on at one grade level and then dropped, however. For example, music curricula in early childhood education help students grasp basic musical concepts intuitively. At subsequent stages the curriculum turns back upon itself at deeper levels of music learning. In this way, a music curriculum explores basic concepts at each level and revisits them in increasing complexity from preschool through high school, in a spiraling pattern.

Music Subject Matter

As was discussed at the beginning of this chapter, music content or subject matter consists of knowledge and skills. Every curriculum format to be discussed here includes both of these because they reflect the nature of music and musical activity. *Knowledge,* the first category of (or theoretical approach to) music content, includes factual or conceptual information about the elements of music, about music history and theory, about musical style, and so forth. The second category includes two types of *skills:* (1) those required for instrumental and vocal performance and (2) those having to do with perceiving musical sound and applying musical knowledge. Unlike performance skills, skills having to do with perception and application of knowledge are not usually acknowledged consciously although they play a crucial role in acquiring musical understanding. The importance of *responses,* the third category of music subject matter, was discussed in Chapter 2. This approach incorporates both knowledge and skills but is more implicit than explicit in curricular structure. Some kind of reaction is evoked by every musical experience, and various kinds of responses result from certain types of interaction with music. Thus, responses to music, like music knowledge and musical skills, must be primary concerns of music educators.

FORMULATING THE CURRICULUM

Levels of Curriculum Development

Official school curricula are formulated at several levels. National and state curriculum recommendations, the broadest and most general level, are partially based on the opinions of professional music education organizations. Where music curriculum is concerned, national or state education recommendations reflect what organizations such as the Music Educators National Conference and the National Association of Schools of Music believe to be the ideal music curriculum for students in U.S. institutions. When formulating recommendations for the state and national levels, these national professional groups consult more specialized organizations of music educators such as the American Choral Directors Association, the American String Teachers Association, and the American School Band Directors Association. Curriculum guides developed by any of these groups usually begin with a general philosophical statement establishing the rationale.

To some extent colleges and universities base their curriculum designs on state and national recommendations. In fact, postsecondary institutions desiring to have their curricula accredited or endorsed must demonstrate compliance with specific recommendations made by state and national organizations. However, these institutions tend to make a greater attempt to accommodate specific needs and interests of their students and faculty.

Similarly, curriculum recommendations formulated by school districts are based on national and state guidelines, but these educational suggestions also consider factors not mentioned in more general program documents in order to accommodate their population's needs and interests. School districts usually publish their curriculum recommendations and make them available to their school administrators and teachers, who in turn use district guides as the foundation for their school's music programs. Teachers then prepare grade-level courses of study from which individual class curricula are derived. By the time curriculum development reaches this stage, it is more or less tailored to specific groups of students or individuals.

This increasing *personalization* accounts for much of the curricular variation among schools and explains some of the marked differences among instructional programs used even with groups or individuals in the same school and at the same grade level. But a second factor, *control,* may contribute more to curricular differences. Recommendations filtered down from the national and state levels through cities and districts to individual schools are recommendations rather than mandates. Teachers and administrators have considerable latitude in implementing these recommendations.

A third factor accounting for curricular differences is procedural. It involves formulating practical solutions to the problem of imparting knowledge and skills. More precisely, it involves *efficiency.* Program designers ideally seek the most direct, least wasteful, and fastest way to convey information to students.

Content, means, and outcomes are the concern of all curricula, regardless of the subject area or the level for which they are developed, and where music is concerned, school programs usually reflect one of six approaches to these three components. Although these approaches overlap somewhat, programs exhibiting most of each approach's characteristics can be identified.

Organizing Subject Matter

The Systems Approach

Many curricula developed by state departments of education, school districts, and universities and a number of those developed by commercial textbook companies are organized around behavioral objectives or goals that describe what students should be able to do as a result of instruction. These *outcome* or *systems approaches* to education are based on answers to four questions: (1) What educational purposes should schools work toward? (2) What experiences can schools provide to make realizing these objectives easier? (3) What is the most effective way to organize these experiences? and (4) What process can be used to determine whether these objectives are being realized?[4]

---

[4] See Ralph Tyler, *Basic Principles of Curriculum and Instruction* (Chicago: University of Chicago Press, 1969).

When applying this system to a music curriculum, teachers must first identify tentative goals that are congruent with music subject matter, with their students' needs (as determined by such characteristics as grade level, age, and prior musical experiences), and with societal, community, and cultural demands. Next, they must evaluate these goals in light of their music education philosophy. This appraisal usually results in goals being revised or eliminated, and the shorter revised list is used for actual curriculum planning. These remaining goals are stated in terms of specific observable student behaviors that will demonstrate when the desired objectives have been realized and to what degree. Then, after identifying or developing activities, materials, and media to facilitate achieving of these objectives, teachers implement their curriculum with students, making changes as necessary to increase its effectiveness. Several such trials and revisions may be necessary before an acceptable program is actually developed.

The Conceptual Approach

The *conceptual approach* to curriculum organization is content centered: Programs are designed so that students acquire general and fundamental understandings about music. This approach is also spiral in that once a foundation of general concepts has been established, more specific concepts about music's elements and characteristics are steadily built on it.

A *concept* is that which remains in the mind after an experience. Stated another way, it is an idea: the knowledge and understanding about things, objects, people, and so forth that one derives from interactions with them. Concepts vary from person to person because these general understandings or ideas about things are experience-based and each person's experiences and mental processes are different. Over time, concepts become quite complex because they represent a synthesis of information gleaned from diverse experiences. This experiential nature of concepts explains why they are continually changing. It also explains why people find it difficult to communicate their concepts verbally and precisely; any explanation or definition of a concept reflects a personal perspective on things or a personal interpretation of events. Thus, concepts cannot be taught directly. Rather, students formulate musical concepts or understandings on the basis of their classroom experiences with music.[5] Experiences can be direct or vicarious. For this reason, knowing and doing work hand in hand in a conceptually conceived curriculum.

Under the conceptual approach, students experience musical concepts in order to learn them, and they apply these same concepts in order to demonstrate learning. Activities allow students to experience concepts about rhythm, melody, form, and so forth, in action—through singing, playing instruments, listening to recordings, reading musical scores, taking dictation, moving to music, and creating music. Reversing this process allows teachers to assess learning. In this manner, students show that learning has taken place by doing something with music. For example, students learn to distinguish between the sound of a violin and the sound of a string bass by listening to and comparing recorded

---

[5] Robert E. Nye, and others, *Music in the Elementary School,* 6th ed. (Englewood Cliffs, NJ: Prentice Hall, 1992), 10.

examples of these instruments. Later in the semester, the teacher plays unfamiliar recordings of these two instruments. As the students listen to these recordings, they give thumbs up if they hear a violin and thumbs down if they hear a string bass. First, the teacher allowed students to experience and formulate concepts of timbre (i.e., the unique sound qualities of violins and string basses) through listening. Then, the teacher used listening to find out what the students had learned: the students did something while listening to demonstrate that they had formulated concepts of timbre.

The Materials Approach

The *materials approach,* in its simplest form, amounts to selecting texts and other instructional materials and building the music program around them or using the curriculum outlined in them. Teachers need only follow the sequence of activities and the procedures recommended in the text or series. Objectives are often stated for each activity so that there is no question about its intended outcome. Frequently, these materials include assessments to assist the teacher with determining whether the objectives have been attained.

In addition to commercial publications, similar curricular materials have been developed by schools districts, states, universities, and educational laboratories. Many of these have been field tested to assure that they accomplish the goals for which they were designed. When carefully and thoughtfully developed, instructional materials are invaluable resources, particularly for inexperienced teachers. They offer a wealth of innovative ideas, and they are somewhat effective with most groups of students because they are developed with average students of a given age and grade level in mind. However, these materials, because of their general nature, necessarily proceed without regard to the needs of specific groups and individual students. Even so, educators usually find that by studying activities and procedures prior to implementing them they can modify experiences and strategies to suit their students' needs and abilities.

The Content Approach

The *music* or *content approach* to curriculum stems from the notion that just as English and literature teachers use great books in the academic curriculum, music educators can use great musical compositions in the music curriculum. Thus, rather than using contrived instructional materials, this fourth approach uses musical works as bases for instruction. Students learn about their instruments and about musical mechanics (i.e., fingerings, time signatures, pitch letter names) while developing the performance skills to overcome practical or technical problems that each composition presents.

In addition, each of these musical compositions presents artistic or interpretive dilemmas, and students acquire musical understanding and gain insight into musical expressiveness as they resolve them. Artistic problems do not usually have clearly defined, specific solutions, so students must do more than use correct fingerings or play correct notes. They must bring all of their musical knowledge and understanding to bear on the problem. A group of students who have learned to sing a madrigal but want to make their performance of it more pleasing face an artistic dilemma. To resolve it, they must use their knowledge about such things as dynamics, phrasing, and balance, and how these and other aspects of music interact to generate pleasing performances. This knowledge generates informed and appropriate decisions about how they can improve their performance.

Under this curricular approach, students learn and apply knowledge and skills immediately, and they are willing to overcome difficult passages because they meet with these passages in the context of beautiful and appropriate music.

This process, then, can lead to desired musical outcomes and develop independent and confident performers while enhancing students' sensitivity to music. Such an approach is especially appropriate for performing ensembles and is most productive when repertoire is selected primarily on the basis of its musical and educational value rather than its appropriateness for the next performance, its utility for festival competitions, or its appeal to a particular audience.

The Activities Approach

Music curricula can be organized around traditional musical behaviors, such as singing, playing instruments, reading and writing music, creating music, moving to music, and listening to recorded or live performances. Active involvement with music through these musical behaviors is the core of this curricular format—hence, the label *activities approach.* In the previous chapter experience was defined as an interaction between the person and the environment; this curricular approach structures classroom environments to heighten in-class musical experiences.

As with the conceptual approach, students' interactions with music in controlled classroom settings lead to knowledge about the nature of the art and about its performance. Specific outcomes and the precise nature of knowledge to be derived from these experiences are not necessarily planned or specified in advance. Consequently, the teacher and student will only have the general intent of an activity in mind before it commences. In this way a single interaction with music can evoke an array of outcomes: All of the students may learn valid and important things, but the specific nature of what they learn will vary considerably within the group.

Because of the open-endedness of this structure, activities must be planned with considerable care so that their musical focus is clear. In addition, although precise learnings and specified objectives may not be set forth, teachers must provide sufficient structure and guidance to ensure that appropriate, desirable, and progressive learning results.

The Method Approach

One frequently hears of vocal music programs that are "Kodály" or "Orff," or of strings and piano programs that are "Suzuki." Such labels usually mean that the precise musical content, the sequence in which it is presented, and the teaching strategies used to convey the content adhere to specifications set forth by the Kodály, Orff, Suzuki, or some other educator. This is the *method approach* to curriculum organization.

This curriculum design is closely related to the activities and conceptual approaches in that it emphasizes learning by doing. Like the materials approach, the method approach offers a prespecified program for educators to follow and, given sufficient attention to other issues such as specific learner needs, this approach can be effective. (Several method curricula are discussed in some detail near the end of Chapter 5.)

COMPREHENSIVE VS. MINIMAL CURRICULUM

Figure 3–1 shows how an ideal school music curriculum is structured. Regardless of the specific way in which content is organized, comprehensive programs will approximate this model. Notice that the curriculum tree has two parts. The first and most important of these, the tree trunk, includes *general music* and *music appreciation courses,* in which factual and conceptual information about music is emphasized. (The primary difference between general music and music appreciation courses is grade level. Music appreciation courses are offered in the high school; general music is offered in elementary, middle, and junior high schools.) Aesthetic sensitivity and musicianship are developed in these classes as students actively participate in a variety of musical experiences, interacting with music and its elements. Activities such as singing, playing instruments, listening to recordings, moving to music, writing music (in dictation or composition), and reading musical notation afford opportunities for students to learn about the elements of music and how they function. Because of these experiences and interactions, learners acquire concepts about music that, in turn, increase their musical understanding, appreciation, and enjoyment.

The branches of the tree are *performance courses,* in which aesthetic sensitivity and musicianship are developed through applied music instruction or instrumental and vocal performance. These courses and ensembles are the second part of the curriculum, and like general music courses, they require that students apply musical knowledge and perceive musical sound. Usually, however, performance-oriented courses use only one mode of interacting with music: Students either sing or play instruments or dance. Seldom do ensembles or instrumental classes explore music through as many modes as do general classes.

This comprehensive, ideal curriculum model is not new, but it remains illusive. Too often one part dominates the curriculum so that the other is slighted. The majority of courses in most secondary school music programs, for instance, focus on performance. In middle schools and high schools in which only a few musical course offerings are possible, these are bound to be performance oriented, even though a large proportion of students enrolled in ensembles lack rudimentary, elementary level musical understanding. General music instruction does not take place in middle, junior high, or high schools unless ensemble directors make it a priority and consciously strive to include general music information and activities in their rehearsals. Similarly, some elementary school programs are so narrowly focused on general music that many young students rarely have the opportunity to work toward and perfect ensemble performance.

In either instance, students are not receiving balanced, well-rounded instruction. They are not receiving a comprehensive music education. Just as branches grow out of a tree trunk as extensions of it, so it must be with performance courses and general music courses. Ultimately, the health of a tree trunk determines the vitality, strength, and growth of the branches.

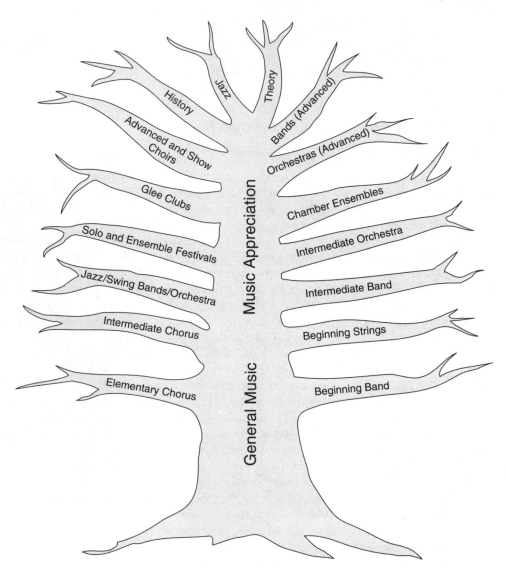

FIGURE 3–1   The Music Curriculum Tree.

Even when teachers have the best intentions, however, circumstances beyond their control may preclude implementing the comprehensive curriculum described here. Inadequate staffing, budget deficits, insufficient time allotments, and the like may limit music instruction. The extent of limitation is an important consideration, but generally, music educators must make the most of whatever situation presents itself. After all, some music instruction may be better than none at all. Or is it?

The answer can only be affirmative if the quality of this minimal instruction offsets other curricular shortcomings. Limited music education experiences are certainly better than none if they lead to increased musical understanding and aesthetic sensitivity. But the value of even this minimal amount of instruction is questionable when it is little more than entertainment, recreation, or diversion from other kinds of courses.

Programs deviating from the two-part comprehensive model should be viewed as one stage in a progression. Music is much more than singing or playing an instrument, no matter how well done. Students who are not given frequent opportunities to develop and expand musical understanding stand little chance of becoming knowledgeable music consumers, yet this is precisely what music education is all about. Some students may continue their music studies and excel in musical performance of some kind, but most are future concert audiences and tape and compact disk buyers—music consumers—whose needs are too often overlooked.

Designing minimal instruction for optimal effect is imperative, and the surest way to structure curriculum for maximum effectiveness is to make those things that are fundamental to musical and aesthetic goals the priority. (See Box 3-1.) General musical knowledge is the foundation on which all other knowledge of the discipline builds. Thus, minimal instruction necessitates basic general music instruction.

When the opportunity arises to improve the music program by adding a course, ex-

---

BOX 3–1   The Comprehensive Music Curriculum

Required Courses
    Required general music, K–6 (or K–8)
    Required unit of fine arts credit for high school graduation, 9–12 (music appreciation, guitar class, music theory, etc.)

Elective Choral Courses
    Elementary chorus
    Middle/junior high school chorus
    High school choirs (SATB, SSA, TTBB, swing, etc.)
    High school solo and ensemble groups

Elective Instrument Courses
    Beginning band or orchestra—heterogeneous groups or beginning like-instrument classes—homogeneous groups
    Intermediate bands and strings
    High school bands and orchestras (jazz/stage bands, chamber ensembles, pep band, marching band)

Elective Nonperformance Classes
    Music history
    Music theory
    Music appreciation
    Electronic music
    Other

panding the content of an existing class, or hiring a new teacher, the improvement should be made in ways that will benefit everyone involved—particularly the largest proportion of students—since curricular deficiencies inevitably result in educational ones. Until such growth and expansion is possible, music educators must make every effort to use minimal resources with maximum efficiency.

STUDY AND DISCUSSION QUESTIONS

1. Explain differences between the goals, teaching strategies, and outcomes of education and schooling as discussed in the Part II introduction. Give specific examples of how music teaching would be handled under each educational approach.
2. Discuss the function of general music education courses. Explain how students entering high school music programs with solid general music backgrounds might be different from others entering the programs without this foundation.
3. What relationships do you see between the ideal music curriculum and the utilitarian philosophy of music education? Between the ideal music curriculum and the aesthetic philosophy of music?
4. In light of your responses to Question 3 and information presented earlier in the text, how would minimal musical instruction affect one's level of music appreciation?
5. Which of the six music curriculum structures might an autonomist use? An expressionist? An absolute expressionist? A formalist? In each instance, justify your answer.

REFERENCES AND RECOMMENDED SOURCES

BRUNER, JEROME. *The Process of Education.* Cambridge: Harvard University Press, 1960; reprint, Cambridge: Harvard University Press, 1977.

————. *Toward A Theory of Instruction.* Cambridge: Harvard University Press, 1966.

FISCHER, LOUIS. "The Constitution and the Curriculum." In *Curriculum Handbook: Administration and Theory.* Ed. by Louis Rubin. Boston: Allyn and Bacon, Inc., 1977.

JACKSON, PHILIP W. "The Student's World." In *Elementary School Journal* 66 (April 1966): 345–57.

NYE, ROBERT E., and others. *Music in the Elementary School.* 6th ed. Englewood Cliffs, NJ: Prentice Hall, 1992.

PETER, G. DAVID, AND ROBERT F. MILLER. *Music Teaching and Learning.* New York: Longman, 1982.

RYLE, GILBERT. "On Knowing How and Knowing That." In *The Concept of Mind.* London: Hutcheson, 1949.

SCHÖN, DONALD A. *Educating the Reflective Practitioner.* The Jossey-Bass Higher Education Series. San Francisco: Jossey-Bass Publishers, 1987.

————. *The Reflective Practitioner: How Professionals Think In Action.* New York: Basic Books, Inc., 1983.

TYLER, RALPH. *Basic Principles of Curriculum and Instruction.* Chicago: University of Chicago Press, 1969.

4

Music Learning

INTRODUCTION AND OBJECTIVES

How do people know that they have learned something? No doubt the answers that come to mind first are some form of the following: (1) They can do something they could not do before, or they do something better; (2) they know something they did not know before, or they know something better; and (3) they appreciate something they did not appreciate before, or they appreciate something more. All of these responses are appropriate and accurate as far as they go. But these responses tell only part of the story.

Any kind of learning, whether it takes place inside or outside of school, is the result of a complex process, even when it appears to come easily or suddenly. Learning never just happens out of the blue; it always has a history. Learning is also developmental, that is, something happens or changes over time. Moreover, regardless of what, how, or where it is being learned, the learner must actively undergo something or learning would not take place. In short, learning is the result of experience in which the learner is actively involved, and it has only occurred if behavior is changed: People know (or feel or do) something that they didn't know (or feel or do) before, or they know (or feel or do) something differently. No matter what the learning, it must lead to a change in behavior. Sometimes this change is immediately overt. Other times, the behavior is covert, as when students think differently from before. Interestingly enough, covert learning always becomes overt at some point. Eventually something done or said will demonstrate that the previous learning occurred. To review: (1) learning is a process, (2) it occurs as a result of experience, (3) it is active in that it only takes place when the mind is actively engaged in the experience, and (4) it leads to a change in behavior.

For years psychologists and theorists have probed this process to understand how learning comes about and to determine what environmental, physical, and psychological conditions make a situation ripe for it, but they have yet to develop a single, unified explanation that applies to all situations equally. Aside from these theories tending to concentrate on one aspect of a multifaceted process, the behaviors that theorists have measured and analyzed really occur after the fact, when some phase of the process evoking them has run its course. Thus, even in light of sophisticated, enlightening, and carefully controlled investigations, the process of learning remains obscure. Steps involved in the sequence called learning can only be conjectured from behaviors signaling that learning has taken place.

Although intricacies of the process are speculative, it is possible to arrive at a logical and reasonably complete picture of learning by examining individual theories and synthesizing the best of them. These are the objectives of this chapter.

Before reading further, however, think of one or two recent personal learning experiences. It doesn't matter what they are. Keep them in mind while reading to see how closely information presented here matches those learning situations.

Information in this chapter will enable readers to do the following:

- Name the major schools of thought about learning and explain their theories.
- Discuss similarities and differences between any two learning theories.
- Define *input, processing, output,* and *feedback* and explain their relationship to the learning process.
- Define *development* and discuss its effects on learning and thinking.
- Name the three domains of learning and describe the type of knowledge and skills in each.
- Tell what the *cybernetic cycle* is and explain how it helps with synthesizing various learning theories.
- Define the term *audiation* and explain its function in music learning.

LEARNING THEORIES

Gestalt and Field Theories

Gestalt theory was introduced in Germany and gained popularity in the United States during the early part of the twentieth century when two of its influential proponents, Wolfgang Köhler (1887–1967) and Kurt Koffka (1886–1941), visited this country after English versions of their writings were published.[1] Undoubtedly, gestalt theory's popularity in the United States was also related to its rebuttal of behaviorist theories that had been developed during the Industrial Revolution. As one writer put it, gestalt theory investigates "the unexpected emergence, from a complex system, of a phenomenon that had not seemed inherent in that system's separate parts. Such 'emergence' or 'collective' phenomena show that 'a whole is more than the sum of its parts.'"[2]

---

[1] Much of the information in this section is found in Gordon H. Bower and Ernest R. Hilgard, *Theories of Learning*, 5th ed. (Englewood Cliffs, NJ: Prentice Hall, 1981).

[2] Marvin Minsky, *The Society of Mind* (New York: Simon and Schuster, Inc., 1986), 328.

It is probably more accurate to say that the whole is different from the sum of its parts. The notion is that the parts taken separately mean something very different from the same parts taken together. According to this theory, people always seek to organize incoming sensory information in the simplest and best manner possible under prevailing conditions. This human tendency to search for the best organization of sensory information, the Law of Prägnanz (also known as the Law of Good Figure or the Law of Good Form), is influenced by several more specific factors, five of which are discussed here.[3]

The Law of Figure-Ground states that people focus on the most prominent aspects of a stimulus and formulate groupings or patterns of those aspects. Those collected features become most important in terms of perceptual organization and stand in relief from any surrounding stimuli. Figure-ground organization accounts in part for the ability to follow a conversation in a noisy restaurant: Important aspects of the conversation stand out as a group from the surrounding noise. It also accounts for the fact that listeners, for example, recognize melodies even in light of transformations such as transposition, dynamic changes, and modal changes. The pattern or grouping of pitches is the most important factor, so that people recognize melodies even when their pitch levels change because the overall pattern remains essentially the same. The theme and variations form is dependent on this kind of pattern recognition.

The Law of Proximity asserts that sensory phenomena are grouped according to their nearness to one another. Things close together in time or space are presumed to be closely related, whereas separated things are less closely related. The strength of these relationships is also a function of proximity. Music reading is easier, then, when notes are spaced according to rhythmic relationships, so that amounts of space allotted for notation should be comparable to duration and should vary with duration.

The Law of Closure or Simplicity, which is closely related to the Law of Proximity, says that people strive to fill gaps in patterns to make them clearer and more stable, which explains the experience known as insight. An unsolved problem amounts to a gap in some existing understanding or body of knowledge; insight occurs when the gap is finally and suddenly filled. It is clear by now that this Aha! feeling does not occur suddenly at all. Rather, it results from a constant reorganizing of elements in the problem situation. Thus, closure refers to perceptual restructuring that leads to a moment when all of the pieces come together and the light goes on. This seemingly instantaneous restructuring is one of the more memorable of all types of learning experiences.

According to a fourth principle, the Law of Contiguity or Common Direction, people tend to group data on the basis of expected direction so that they perceive continuous patterns rather than disconnected ones. A series of disconnected straight lines, for instance, may appear as a square, and a collection of separate curved lines may become a complete circle. With musical sound, a series of pitches or a progression of sounds with indefinite pitch are heard as melodies and rhythm patterns, not as separate, unrelated pitches or sounds.

---

[3] See Willis D. Ellis, *A Source Book of Gestalt Psychology,* with an introduction by Kurt Koffka (London: Routledge and Kegan Paul, 1938) for historical information about gestalt psychology and for in-depth information about each of the perception laws presented here. This reference also contains writings by Köhler and Koffka.

Finally, the Law of Similarity explains why students with limited musical experience often have difficulty distinguishing among the sounds of various instruments, particularly when these instruments are playing together. This principle also helps to explain why inner voices in a musical piece are sometimes so difficult for students to hear and follow. The law states that phenomena that are similar in color, shape, texture, form, and the like will be grouped together.

From this discussion, it is clear that gestaltists' investigations center on how people organize data in order to process them. Gestaltists maintain that perceptual organization processes are genetic, but research suggests that they improve with training, as does any aptitude, so that one learns to use the processes more selectively and skillfully. In addition, gestalt theorists have a good deal to say about how people organize information to facilitate memory.

Field theory, a derivative of gestalt theory, combines gestalt theories about perceptual organization with physics notions about magnetic fields to explain relationships between perception and memory. These theories emphasize the role of motivation or "drive" in initiating and directing purposive behavior.

James Mursell, for instance, wrote extensively about music education and musical growth in classroom settings.[4] He was keenly aware of the student's role in learning, and he believed that, unless students are intrinsically motivated to learn, their musical growth will be minimal at best. To Mursell's way of thinking, the best motivator is the active, participatory musical experience—singing, playing, listening to, and being actively involved in other ways with high-quality music. This is the all-important starting point for motivation, and it is from these experiences that musical growth can be drawn.

He applies his "synthesis-analysis-synthesis" or whole-part-whole pattern of learning to music learning and speaks of musical understanding as "unfolding or evolving, rather than adding or accumulating."[5] Instead of teaching the rudiments of music in isolation from the musical contexts that give them meaning, Mursell suggests that factual knowledge about music will gradually be drawn from songs that students have learned and enjoy singing. Each time they sing a particular song, they do something different with it and learn a little bit more about it. In this way their understanding of melody, rhythm, dynamics, and so forth deepens gradually as an outgrowth of meaningful music making rather than of drill and practice. At the end of each such activity, when students sing the song through once more, it means more to them than it did prior to the "analysis" or unfolding of it.

Cognitive Theories

Cognitive theories of learning are closely related to gestalt and field theories because they are also interested in what people do with sensory information. They hypothesize that mental structures—concepts, principles, and schema, for instance—enable learners to re-

[4] James L. Mursell, *Music and Education: Principles and Programs* (Morristown, NJ: Silver Burdett Co., 1956).
[5] Ibid., 79.

tain information, that is, remember, in an organized manner. These structures are formulated on the basis of perceived relationships among individual facts and bits of information. Therefore, memory, a crucial element in learning, is aided by one's ability to discern such relationships.

Bruner's spiral curriculum generally follows this structure. As students progress through school, they constantly receive new data that must be stored and accessed. General conceptual foundations that Bruner suggests be established during the early years of schooling serve as ready-made "holding tanks" for this information.

Ausubel, another prominent cognitive theorist, defines cognitive structure as "the substantive content of a particular subject-matter area or sub area at any given time, and its organization, stability, and clarity."[6] His investigations of verbal learning emphasize the important role that "advance organizers" play in memory and learning. These abstract, general, and conceptual organizers are key ideas that are presented before new material is introduced. Like Bruner's concepts, Ausubel's organizers "anchor" the new information by providing a structure within which it can be subsumed (expository organizers) or by helping students recall something they already know so that new material can immediately be related to it (comparative organizers). In either case, learners have a place to file incoming data for short- or long-term storage.

"Chunking" describes one mental process used when grouping data for storage and easy retrieval. This process may be applied to small and large groups of information and to knowledge as well as technical skills. For example, rather than depending on discrete bits of aural, verbal, or motor learnings, music students rely on concepts and patterns of behaviors to help them solve musical problems.

Recently, cognitive psychologists have begun using the computer as the model for the learning process. Johnson-Laird's definition of learning as being "the construction of new programs out of the elements of experience" is very similar to one set forth by Hart, who defines learning as "the acquisition of useful programs."[7] In both instances, patterns of cognition and behavior are central to the learning process, although Hart, like Mursell, emphasizes the function of motivation in learning. He believes that schooling should help students acquire groups of skills that they view as useful for achieving personal self-determined goals.

Metacognition Theory

Metacognition, or thinking about thinking, focuses on self-knowledge—of mental abilities, mental states, and of self-regulating strategies.[8] Learners who recognize that they do not know something, who are aware that they remember things better when they

---

[6] See David Ausubel, *The Psychology of Meaningful Verbal Learning and Retention* (New York: Greene and Stratton, 1963).

[7] Philip N. Johnson-Laird, *The Computer and the Mind* (Cambridge: Harvard University Press, 1988), 133; Leslie Hart, *Human Brain and Human Learning* (New York: Longman Inc., 1983), 86.

[8] Information about this theory is taken from Scott G. Parris and Barbara K. Lindauer, "The Development of Cognitive Skills during Childhood." Transcript in the hands of the authors.

write them down, or who have decided that a particular method of studying works best for them are demonstrating metacognitive behavior. In each instance, what the learners know about their mental functioning—in essence, what they know about how they think—is the basis for the goal-directed or purposive behavior required in learning.

Research suggests that metacognitive ability develops between ages five and eight, the period that numerous theorists have identified as a critical one in cognitive development. Some of these postulations are discussed in detail in the "Developmental Theories" section, but in general terms this is the period during which children move from perceptual and extrinsically governed thought processes to conceptual and reflective or intrinsically regulated processes.

Erik Erikson's psychosocial development theory relates to the development of self-knowledge or metacognition. He used clinical observations to determine how one's personality and sense of identity develop. More specifically, his investigations focused on cultural and social factors affecting the development of the conscious self or the ego. Generally, Erikson found that throughout life, people move through a series of eight developmental stages. A specific task characterizes each stage and must be mastered in order for development to move forward; failure to complete any of the tasks interferes with development at later stages. The onset of these stages is determined by maturation and by societal or cultural demands so that their actual beginning or end may vary from one culture to another. In addition, a person's ability to move through each level successfully is dependent on the nature of his or her interaction with others—parents, peers, teachers.

Self-knowledge theories have far-reaching implications for learning because they emphasize the student's role in a way not found in other theories. To begin with, these theories are related to self-esteem, a psychological construct "concerned with whether or not people evaluate themselves in a positive manner, and if so, the strength of their positive self-attitudes."[9] In turn, self-esteem relates to personal attributes such as assertiveness, independence, and instrumental competence, and each of these relates to one's sense of having some control over self and the environment and one's ability to achieve.

If, as research suggests, metacognition is one basis for constructing plans to facilitate learning, and if metacognitive planning is essentially the deliberate selection of strategies for realizing goals, it is realistic to expect that, all other things being equal, learning will only be as good as self-knowledge allows. This is especially pertinent to music learning involving regular practice sessions because such sessions are almost always self-directed. Under these conditions, metacognitive assessments of knowledge, understanding, skill, performance, and most effective remedial strategies become extremely important.

---

[9] William Damon, *Social and Personality Development: Infancy through Adolescence* (New York: W. W. Norton and Co., 1983), 225.

Behavioral Theories

The term *behaviorism* was coined by John B. Watson in 1914.[10] He argued that psychologists should focus on overt and measurable behaviors rather than on covert, subjective, and introspective types of behavior, which dominated psychological thought then. Ivan Pavlov's classical conditioning, involving reinforcement and extinction, and Edward L. Thorndike's connectionism[11] are noteworthy early examples of concern with overt behavior. These men and other early behaviorists interested in studying behavior scientifically investigated it through stimulus-response laboratory research, which deemphasized the mind as a mediating variable or bypassed this notion of mind entirely.

Behaviorists see learning as a process of linking actions and consequences together in stimulus-response bonds. Similarly, perception is made up of groups of stimulus-response associations. For example, music teachers provide a stimulus such as a verbal command or a conducting gesture, and students respond with the appropriate or conditioned behavior—sitting or standing with correct posture, raising their instruments into playing position, reducing the level of classroom noise, and so forth.

As a rule, obtaining the initial appropriate response from students is much easier than getting them to maintain it.[12] This aspect of behaviorism was B. F. Skinner's primary concern. In his effort to sustain these responses, Skinner conducted research applying Thorndike's Law of Effect, which says that when responses to a given stimulus are associated with, or followed closely by, satisfying outcomes or rewards, they become more firmly connected with that stimulus and are strengthened. Conversely, responses associated with dissatisfying outcomes or nonrewards are more loosely connected with the stimulus and are weakened.

Skinner's application of Thorndike's law introduced two additional behavioral techniques. The first of these is contingent reinforcement, which shapes behavior in an active rather than passive way. Here, an "if-then" relationship exists between a given behavior and its outcome; the behavior is followed by reinforcement instead of being elicited or induced by it. Next, rather than defining reinforcement as some type of reward, Skinner viewed it more comprehensively as any consequence that increases the frequency of a behavior.

By viewing reinforcement in this general way, Skinner shed light on the acting-out behavior that is so common in educational settings and provided insight about other types of chronically inappropriate, even self-destructive, types of behavior. Children who desire or need attention discover that they get this attention if they behave in certain ways. Thus,

---

[10] See John B. Watson, "Psychology as the Behaviorist Views It," *Psychological Review* 20 (1913), 158–177; reprint, *Psychological Review* 101 (1994), 248–253; and John B. Watson, *Behaviorism,* rev. ed. (New York: W. W. Norton and Co., 1930).

[11] See Edward L. Thorndike, *Animal Intelligence* (New York: Macmillan, 1911); and I. P. Pavlov, *Pavlov: Selected Works,* trans. S. Belsky (Moscow: Foreign Languages Publishing House, 1955).

[12] See B. F. Skinner, *Science and Human Behavior* (New York: Macmillan, 1953); and B. F. Skinner, *Beyond Freedom and Dignity* (New York: Bantam Books, 1971).

although their behavior may lead to unpleasant, embarrassing, or harmful consequences, it continues because any attention to it reinforces it.

According to Skinner, reinforcement is a most efficient means of perpetuating desired behavior. In addition, scheduling reinforcement (or applying it in the ways described by his concepts of shaping, fading, extinction, positive and negative reinforcement, and punishment) potentially allows considerable control over student learning. Scheduling also provides a means by which learner behavior may gradually become less dependent on reinforcement. (See Table 4–1 for types of positive and negative reinforcement.)

Developmental Theories

One point must be clarified before discussing developmental theories. When learning theorists refer to cognitive or psychomotor skills as being developmental, they mean that something happens over time. But behaviors that occur because people get older or because time passes are different from those being discussed here. There are some things that people cannot or do not do, not because they don't want to do them but because they are not physically or mentally ready and able to do them. No matter how long or hard someone works at "teaching" youngsters to execute behaviors such as walking and talking, for example, they will be physically and mentally unable to do them until they are *developmentally* ready—until their mental and physical abilities have developed to a point where they *can* do them. Simply stated, these behaviors and others like them cannot be "taught" and are not "learned" in the same way that math or spelling or chemistry behaviors are taught and learned.

TABLE 4–1   Classroom Applications of Reinforcement (Derived from Skinner's Contingency Theory of Reinforcement)

Positive Reinforcement	Positive Punishment
Add a reward: give something needed, wanted, welcomed Primary reinforcement—basic needs Secondary reinforcement*—learned wants (star, medal, candy, verbal praise)	Add an undesirable stimulus: give something unpleasant, unwanted, unwelcome (spank, yell, scold, reduce grade, take away free time)
Negative Reinforcement	Negative Punishment
Remove an undesirable stimulus, or remove the individual from an undesirable situation (release a student from study hall to go practice; stop reminding a student to do a task once it's completed; excuse a student from auditions for getting a high rating at festival)	Remove something that serves as a reward, something the learner wishes to keep (do not allow a student to play because he/she misbehaved or failed an exam)

*Note that some things teachers think are positive reinforcers may not be and that some punishments may be positive reinforcers.

Jean Piaget's Theory of Cognitive Development

Whereas behaviorists focus on external causes of human behavior, cognitive theorists are more interested in determining how mental functioning develops over time and how its development affects perception and learning. Their theories focus on input and process. Jean Piaget, perhaps the most widely known cognitive psychologist, initially watched his children complete various tasks and questioned them about the task and about their perception of things. He later conducted similar research with other youngsters.

As a result of this research, Piaget theorized that major shifts in cognitive functioning accompany dramatic changes in the way people understand and interact with their environment. Human beings constantly seek a state of *equilibration,* a time when everything in their world makes sense: They are, in effect, in balance with their surroundings. When some new thing enters that world and does not find a match with something that is already there, people are temporarily thrown into a state of *disequilibrium,* and the only way out of this state is to find a way of blending the new with the known. This blending involves *assimilation* (taking in new data and trying to make sense of it) and *accommodation* (modifying existing cognitive structures so that this new information fits in). Once this is done, equilibration is regained, but the cognitive structures or schemas are forever changed by the experience.[13]

According to Piaget, human beings develop through four distinct stages, each characterized by a specific way of acquiring, organizing, and applying knowledge of the environment. The names of these stages reflect their relationship to operational (abstract, internal, or reflective) thought: (1) the *sensorimotor* stage, a "pre-thought" period from birth to two years of age; (2) *the preoperational* stage, from two years until approximately age seven; (3) the *concrete operations* stage, which lasts from age seven until approximately age twelve or thirteen; and (4) the *formal operations* stage, approximately age thirteen and beyond. According to this stage theory, children are mentally unable to engage in abstract thought processes until the end of the third stage, at approximately age twelve.[14]

Each stage is marked by a specific mental deficiency that must be overcome before the next stage can begin and development of abstract thinking ability can progress. The first challenges facing developing children are overcoming egocentrism (a tendency to fixate on particular aspects of stimuli accompanied by an inability to imagine things being any other way) and acquiring object permanence (the internal representation of an object, which enables children to understand that things exist even though they are out of sight). Preoperational children must acquire various types of conservation abilities, which allow them to hold attributes of objects constant across various other changes in their form. Finally, children at the concrete operations stage must attain reversibility—the ability to reverse actions mentally, a primary ability required for abstract thought such as hypothesizing and systematic problem solving. At each level, overcoming the cognitive obstacle

---

[13] See Jean Piaget, *The Construction of Reality in the Child,* trans. Margaret Cook (New York: Basic Books, 1954); and Howard E. Gruber and J. Jacques Vonèche, *The Essential Piaget* (New York: Basic Books, 1977).

[14] Ibid.

marks a step in a progression away from dependence on external or concrete representations of the world and toward internalized, reflective, and abstract representations.[15]

Piaget's ideas have been subjected to considerable criticism in recent years for several reasons. In addition to those who criticize his lack of experimental control and scientific rigor or his reliance on children's limited verbal abilities, others believe that his stage theory is at least partially incorrect or that he is wrong about how mental skills develop. Still others suggest that factors such as prior experience and expertise are primary determinants of one's ability to execute specific Piagetian tasks, regardless of the subject's age. Even so, these ideas remain among the most influential ones in educational theory, primarily because of the insight they provide about children's mental abilities and because numerous other psychologists, educators, and theorists have replicated his studies and reached similar conclusions.

Theorists who have replicated Piaget's experiments using musical tasks have discovered parallels between mental development and the development of certain musical perception and performance skills. Marilyn Pflederer Zimmerman was the first to use musical tasks in order to investigate Piaget's theory of conservation. Her preliminary work supported the notion that, prior to age seven or eight, children have difficulty conserving or recognizing melodies in light of changes to their meter, rhythm, or tone quality. Zimmerman's subsequent studies and other studies inspired by her groundbreaking work also support, or rather do not disprove, Piaget's conservation theory as it relates to musical tasks involving melody, rhythm and harmony, and a number of other musical elements.[16]

Bruner's Theory of Cognitive Development

Some of Jerome Bruner's ideas have already been mentioned several times in this text.[17] Like Piaget, for whose work he had a great deal of respect, Bruner was concerned with the internal origins of cognitive behavior and with intellectual development. His theory is based on "benchmarks" about the nature of cognitive growth, all having to do with the gradual development of increasingly abstract thought processes.

Bruner offers three stages of mental development and believes that people think about, understand, interact with, and remember aspects of their environment in markedly different ways during each stage. Thus, the three levels are named for the type of representation they utilize. The first of these stages is called *enactive* because mental functioning during this period centers around action or doing and is governed by learned responses and habituation. In the *iconic* stage, which develops next, representation "depends upon visual or other sensory organization and upon the use of summarizing images."[18] In other words, iconic mental functioning is governed by principles similar to those associated with gestalt theory. Finally, the *symbolic* stage enables people to use symbols such as words and symbol systems such as language to convey, recall, and acquire understanding of their en-

[15] Ibid.

[16] David J. Hargreaves, *The Developmental Psychology of Music* (Cambridge: Cambridge University Press, 1986), 43–50.

[17] See Jerome Bruner, *Toward a Theory of Instruction* (Cambridge, MA: Belknap Press, 1966).

[18] Ibid., 10–11.

vironment on an abstract level. In addition, people can mentally manipulate or transpose these symbols to generate a plethora of hypothetical or imaginary "environments," all of which can be understood and envisioned via symbol systems.

One additional thing to note is Bruner's emphasis on the development of "self-accounting" or "self-consciousness"—a capability referred to earlier as metacognition. He believes that this ability frees learners from adaptive behavior by enabling them to engage in introspective and reflective behaviors such as logic and reasoning. Accordingly, he maintains that

> mental growth is in very considerable measure dependent upon growth from the outside in—a mastering of techniques that are embodied in the culture and that are passed on in a contingent dialogue by agents of the culture. . . . It is this that leads me to think that the heart of the educational process consists of providing aids and dialogues for translating experience into more powerful systems of notation and ordering.[19]

The Cybernetic Cycle

The term *cybernetics* derives from the Greek *kybernetes,* meaning a steersman, a helmsman, or pilot and indicating the ability to "stay on course" or reach a goal. As developed by mathematician Norbert Wiener, the *cybernetic cycle,* an information processing model, draws similarities between checks-and-balances systems (such as those used in computer programs) and the self-monitoring function of the human mind.[20] "Artificial intelligence" built into automated mechanisms simulates sensory processes that guide goal-directed human behavior by constantly providing corrective information to its steersmen, that is, the mind and the nervous system. People achieve goals, then, because purposive behavior is guided by *feedback.*

Wiener's cybernetic cycle is shown in Figure 4–1. Notice that sensory information related to a desired outcome is received (input unit), then processed and stored in memory (process unit). On the basis of this stored information, tentative decisions are made about which strategy will help to achieve a desired outcome (output unit), and a plan is implemented. While executing this plan, or shortly thereafter, consequences of each action provide information (1) confirming the strategy, (2) providing data about improving it, or (3) suggesting that a different strategy be chosen (feedback unit). The cycle then begins again.

Think for a minute about how people practice music. They play or sing a passage and store this performance or input in memory. Then they evaluate the stored performance, and on the basis of this analysis, they modify it or attempt to sustain or repeat it. Their input units (ears, eyes, muscles, or teacher's comments) send signals about the performance

---

[19] Ibid., 21.

[20] See Norbert Wiener, *Cybernetics,* 2d ed. (Cambridge: M. I. T. Press, 1961); and Norbert Wiener, *The Human Use of Human Beings* (Boston: Houghton Mifflin, 1954; reprint, The Da Capo Series in Science, New York: Da Capo Press, 1988).

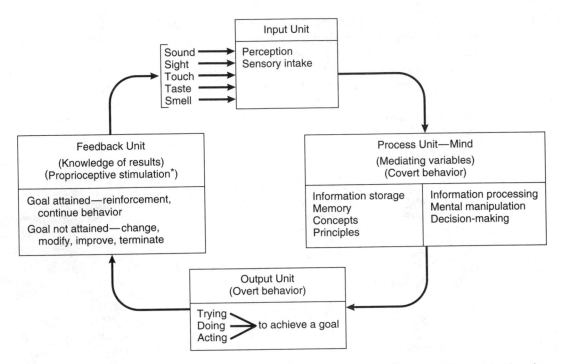

*Muscle feel and kinesthetic responses provide knowledge of results (feedback) that is vital to musical learning. Feedback and new sensory input that the learner receives during subsequent cycles guide the learning process and serve as bases for new decisions.

FIGURE 4-1   The cybernetic cycle.   *Source:* Adapted from Joseph A. Labuta, *Guide to Accountability in Music Instruction* (West Nyack, NY: Parker Publishing Company, 1974), 26.

to the brain—the processing unit—and this prompts output (they do something), which they continue or change based on its results (the feedback unit). And so the model goes.

Although not intended to be a model of learning, Wiener's information processing model seems to illustrate the chain of events involved in learning. In fact, most learning theories focus on one or two of the four units in the cycle—input, processing, output, and feedback. Gestalt psychologists are particularly interested in how the mind organizes perceived sensory information in order to process it. Thus, they concentrate almost exclusively on the input unit of the cybernetic cycle. Skinner's and other behaviorists' work related to conditioning responses focuses on the output and feedback dimensions of the cycle. Cognitive theorists, in contrast, focus upon the process unit of the cybernetic cycle, although they are most concerned with information storage and memory.

This cybernetic cycle may be the only comprehensive model of learning because it encompasses all aspects of the goal-directed behavior involved in learning. For this reason, it offers a framework for comparing schools of learning psychology and theories of learning while providing a fairly complete picture of the learning process.

LEARNING STYLES

Any group of learners includes students who acquire and retain information best when it is presented in one of four different ways or styles. Some students are *auditory* learners. They learn best by listening and talking with their teachers and peers. These students enjoy discussions, group work, and cooperative learning projects. Other students are *visual* learners who would rather read, analyze, follow written directions, and the like. A third group of students are *kinesthetic* learners who learn best when they do something physical. They like to interact with instructional materials—to touch, manipulate, and examine things. A fourth group of students are more *intuitive* and open-ended in their approach to learning. These students prefer to discover things rather than being told about them. Given an option, they would probably choose experimentation over didactic instruction.

Several researchers have moved beyond these relatively simple descriptions of learning styles. Anthony F. Gregorc, for instance, studied successful learners and discovered that (1) their learning style is a function of the manner in which they perceive and process information and (2) their way of perceiving and processing information varies depending on the context in which it is received. According to his theory,[21] there are two ways of perceiving: *Concrete perception* occurs through the physical senses, whereas *abstract perception* occurs via the intellect, imagination, and emotions. (The text has referred to these as direct and vicarious experience, respectively.) In addition, Gregorc describes two ways of processing information. *Sequential processing* is the tendency to handle information in a linear, highly structured, step-by-step manner. *Random processing* is multidimensional and characterized by intuitive leaps and the use of exploratory strategies.

By pairing these ways of perceiving and processing, Gregorc identifies four broad learning styles: concrete/sequential, abstract/sequential, concrete/random, and abstract/random. Concrete/sequential learners are well-organized, efficient, and task oriented. They tend to do well with structured drill and practice, hands-on projects, and computer-assisted learning. Abstract/sequential learners enjoy thinking about topics and situations and analyzing data to extract important ideas. They usually have well-developed writing and language skills and learn well from lectures and extensive reading. Concrete/random learners are task takers. They prefer to work independently—on experiments, on computers and games, and on problem-solving tasks. Finally, abstract/random learners tend to be imaginative, divergent, and flexible in their approach to learning. They prefer open-ended, unstructured presentations and usually do well in art, music, and other creative activities. They enjoy working in groups because they tend to be sensitive to the atmosphere and nuances of situations.

Most teachers teach the way they prefer to learn, but those who are sensitive to their personal learning style and to learning-style differences among their students will use a variety of teaching methods so that they reach every learner. This broad view of learning, when reflected in teaching, helps to avoid a good deal of frustration for everyone involved.

---

[21] See Anthony F. Gregorc, "Learning/Teaching Styles: Their Nature and Effects," in National Association of Secondary School Principals, *Student Learning Styles: Diagnosing and Prescribing Programs* (Washington DC: National Association of Secondary School Principals, 1979); and Anthony F. Gregorc, *Inside Styles: Beyond the Basics* (Maynard, MA: Gabriel Systems, 1985).

TYPES OF LEARNING

Some years ago, curriculum specialists and researchers who recognized that learning is not a simple unitary process differentiated learnings or behaviors that are primarily intellectual (cognitive), those that are primarily physical (motor), and those that are primarily emotional (affective) and categorized them accordingly. The three domains of learning that resulted were each arranged from the simplest or most basic learning to the most complex. Such an arrangement is called a *taxonomy*.

Separating different kinds of learning in this way facilitates analysis, study, lesson planning, and clarity, but ultimately, this separation is artificial. None of these taxonomies provides a true picture of learning when isolated from the others. Figure 4–2 illustrates interrelationships among the three kinds of learning. Students learn subject-matter by doing something with it, and in the process of learning they grow to like or dislike the subject matter, the task, or both.

With this caution in mind about the potential danger of artificial separation, note that objectives used for instructional planning tend to emphasize one or another of these three types of learning. Cognitive objectives emphasize thinking and other mental processes. Psychomotor objectives focus on physical skills and techniques. Affective objectives are concerned with feelings, attitudes, emotions, and appreciation. Figure 4–3 shows the three taxonomies with their levels of learning complexity. Tables 4–2, 4–3, and 4–4 provide appropriate actions for various levels in each hierarchy. Most music objectives can be classified as (1) verbal/cognitive, (2) aural/cognitive, (3) psychomotor, or (4) affective. These categories are the basis for planning, teaching, and evaluating music courses.

Verbal/cognitive objectives relate to knowledge and the mental processes associated with it. They require recognition, recall, and classification of music symbols, music vocabulary, and information about musical elements, forms, styles, and so forth. Although certain concepts and information are essential for music learning, teachers must guard against overemphasizing objectives at the lowest levels of cognitive learning, especially those involving the memorization of facts. Information is essential only for its use. Thus, verbal/cognitive objectives should be evaluated in light of the levels of complexity for which they are set.

Aural/cognitive objectives require applying verbal/cognitive knowledge in order to classify musical sound. In general, they represent a higher level of processing, one that requires discriminating listening. Students must classify what they hear in music on the ba-

FIGURE 4-2   Three interrelated domains of learning.   *Source:* Adapted from Joseph A. Labuta, *Guide to Accountability in Music Instruction* (West Nyack, NY: Parker Publishing Company, 1974; copyright assigned to Joseph A. Labuta, 1991), 48.

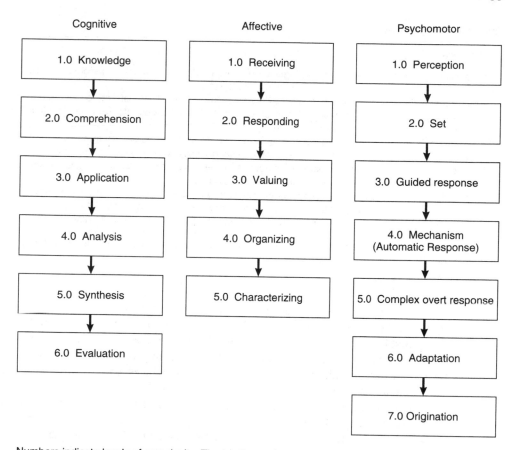

Numbers indicate levels of complexity. The least complex actions are numbers 1.0.

FIGURE 4-3   Three-part taxonomic scheme for instructional objectives.   *Source:* Adapted from Benjamin S. Bloom, and others, *A Taxonomy of Educational Objectives: Handbook I, The Cognitive Domain* (New York: Longman, Green, and Co., 1965); David R. Krathwohl, and others, *A Taxonomy of Educational Objectives: Handbook II, The Affective Domain* (New York: David Mackay Co., 1964); and Elizabeth J. Simpson, *The Classification of Educational Objectives,* Report No. OE5–85–104 (Washington, DC: U.S. Office of Education, 1966).

sis of what they know about music. These aural/cognitive abilities are essential for music consumers and performers.

   Psychomotor objectives require applying knowledge through physical responses such as singing, playing instruments, moving to music, and reading notation. Note that music reading might also be classified as a cognitive skill and is frequently taught in the same way that historical facts about music are taught. Ultimately, however, teaching rhythmic or melodic reading effectively requires movement, physical sensations, and actual performance.

Table 4-2   **Cognitive Domain**

Classification	Examples of Behavioral Descriptors
1.0 Knowledge	to define, to distinguish, to know, to identify, to recall, to recognize, to be conscious of, to match, to memorize, to listen for
2.0 Comprehension	to describe in one's own words, to translate, to transform, to illustrate, to change, to restate, to interpret, to rearrange, to demonstrate, to name (label), to explain, to express, to locate
3.0 Application	to apply, to generalize, to choose, to organize, to use, to transfer, to restructure, to classify, to order (arrange in sequence), to dramatize, to illustrate
4.0 Analysis	to discriminate, to categorize, to perceive, to deduce, to analyze, to compare, to describe, to differentiate, to diagram
5.0 Synthesis	to write, to produce, to create, to originate, to design, to modify, to develop, to formulate, to construct, to compose, to plan, to manipulate
6.0 Evaluation	to judge, to evaluate, to appraise, to consider, to weigh, to rate

Adapted from Benjamin S. Bloom, and others, *A Taxonomy of Educational Objectives: Handbook I, The Cognitive Domain* (New York: Longman, Green, and Co., 1956).

Affective objectives include some of the most important outcomes of the music program, but they are difficult to state in behavioral terms and are more difficult to measure. How do students look or what do students do if they appreciate and love music? This knotty problem will be tackled in the next chapter, but in general, objectives in this domain have to do with attitudes toward music, musical preferences, emotive responses to music, and aesthetic sensitivity.

Music teachers use the these taxonomies to make certain that, when taken together, instructional objectives represent a balanced program and encompass all types and levels of learning. The wording of the objectives in each domain tells what learner behavior (action) is required. The prescribed action also indicates the level of cognitive, psychomotor, or affective learning. Look at the cognitive domain chart in Table 4–2 for a moment. Note that for verbal/cognitive and aural cognitive learning, students may be asked to define, illustrate, apply, analyze, create, or evaluate. Each of these behaviors represents a more sophisticated level of cognition. Objectives requiring the higher cognitive processes of syn-

Table 4-3   **Affective Domain**

Classification	Examples of Behavioral Descriptors
1.0 Receiving	to accept, to share, to listen, to select
2.0 Responding	to approve, to volunteer, to applaud, to spend leisure time in, to acclaim
3.0 Valuing	to support, to join, to appreciate, to debate, to argue, to choose
4.0 Organizing	to discuss, to abstract, to define, to formulate, to design
5.0 Characterizing	to revise, to change, to complete, to be rated high by peers in, to be rated high by music teachers in, to resolve

Adapted from David R. Krathwohl, and others, *A Taxonomy of Educational Objectives: Handbook II, The Affective Domain* (New York: David Mackay Co., 1964).

Table 4–4   Psychomotor Domain

Classification	Examples of Behavioral Descriptors
1.0 Perception	to hear, to see, to sense, to relate to action
2.0 Set	to be ready, to be adjusted for performance
3.0 Guided Response	to carry out an act with guidance, to perform with supervision
4.0 Mechanism (Automatic Response)	to respond from habit, to have some skill in performance
5.0 Complex Overt Response	to have high degree of skill in performance, to be efficient in response, to perform complex patterns, to perform without hesitation, to perform a finely coordinated skill with ease
6.0 Adaptation	to modify an act as required by setting or context, to adjust performance with ease
7.0 Origination	to develop a new performance pattern or skill, to combine performance patterns in unique ways

Adapted from Elizabeth J. Simpson, *The Classification of Educational Objectives,* Report No. OE5–85–104 (Washington, DC: U. S. Office of Education, 1966).

thesis and evaluation might read: Student will *create* a short composition in rondo form; or students will *evaluate* a composer's use of ternary form.

This chapter has explored learning and noted that it is a complex process occurring over time. Chapter 3 discussed music curriculum and set forth general knowledge and skills that students must learn in order to benefit from music education. In Chapter 5 the music teacher's task, which is to help students acquire this general knowledge and skills, is the focus.

STUDY AND DISCUSSION QUESTIONS

1. Prepare an oral or written report about one person in the following list. The presentation should (a) discuss the person's ideas about learning and explain their relationship to the cybernetic cycle; (b) explain ways in which the person's ideas were innovative or traditional at the time they were introduced; and (c) discuss similarities and differences between this person's ideas and at least two theories discussed in this chapter.
    Maria Montessori (1870-1952)   Rudolf Steiner (1861–1925)
    Robert M. Gagné (1916–)   Johann F. Herbart (1776–1841)
    G. Stanley Hall (1844–1924)   Jean-Jacques Rousseau (1712–1778)

2. Is the technical level of a person's performance an accurate indication of his or her musical knowledge? Of his or her musical understanding? Why, or why not?

3. Do technical accuracy and musicality or expressiveness reveal the same things about the performer's musical understanding and knowledge? Explain your answer.

4. What function, if any, does metacognition serve in applied music instruction, particularly in practice sessions away from the teacher's studio? Is that function the same for instrumentalists and vocalists? Explain your response.

5. (a) Would a formalist approach to music instruction favor one learning style more than another? Would a referential approach? Would an expressionist approach? (b) Would any
of these approaches work better than the others for developing a specific kind of learning (cognitive, affective or psychomotor)? Elaborate on your answer.

REFERENCES AND RECOMMENDED SOURCES

AUSUBEL, DAVID.   *The Psychology of Meaningful Verbal Learning and Retention.* New
York: Greene and Stratton, 1963.

BLOOM, BENJAMIN, AND OTHERS.   *A Taxonomy of Educational Objectives: Handbook I,
The Cognitive Domain.* New York: Longman, Green, and Co., 1956.

BOWER, GORDON H., AND ERNEST R. HILGARD.   *Theories of Learning.* 5th ed. Englewood
Cliffs, NJ: Prentice-Hall, 1981.

BRUNER, JEROME.   *Toward a Theory of Instruction.* Cambridge, MA: Belknap Press,
1966.

DAMON, WILLIAM.   *Social and Personality Development: Infancy through Adolescence,*
New York: W. W. Norton and Co., 1983.

ELLIS, WILLIS D.   *A Source Book of Gestalt Psychology.* With an introduction by Kurt
Koffka. London: Routledge and Kegan Paul, 1938.

GREGORC, ANTHONY F.   *Inside Styles: Beyond the Basics.* Maynard, MA: Gabriel Systems, 1985.

———.   "Learning/Teaching Styles: Their Nature and Effects." In *Student Learning
Styles: Diagnosing and Prescribing Programs.* Washington, DC: National Association of Secondary School Principals, 1979.

GRUBER, HOWARD E., AND J. JACQUES VONÈCHE.   *The Essential Piaget.* New York: Basic
Books, 1977.

HARGREAVES, DAVID J.   *The Developmental Psychology of Music.* Cambridge: Cambridge University Press, 1986.

HART, LESLIE.   *Human Brain and Human Learning.* New York: Longman Inc., 1983.

JOHNSON-LAIRD, PHILIP N.   *The Computer and the Mind.* Cambridge: Harvard University
Press, 1988.

KRATHWOHL, DAVID R., AND OTHERS.   *A Taxonomy of Educational Objectives: Handbook
II, The Affective Domain.* New York: David Mackay's Co., 1964.

LABUTA, JOSEPH A.   *Guide to Accountability in Music Instruction.* West Nyack, NY:
Parker Publishing Co., 1974; copyright assigned to Joseph A. Labuta, 1991.

MINSKY, MARVIN.   *The Society of Mind.* New York: Simon and Schuster, Inc., 1986.

MURSELL, JAMES L. *Music and Education: Principles and Programs.* Morristown, NJ: Silver Burdett Co., 1956.

PARRIS, SCOTT G., AND BARBARA K. LINDAUER.   "The Development of Cognitive Skills
During Childhood." Transcript in possession of the authors.

PAVLOV, I. P.   *Pavlov: Selected Works.* Trans. S. Belsky. Moscow: Foreign Languages
Publishing House, 1955.

PIAGET, JEAN.   *The Construction of Reality in the Child.* Trans. Margaret Cook. New
York: Basic Books, 1954.

SIMPSON, ELIZABETH J. *The Classification of Educational Objectives.* Report No. OE5–85–104. Washington, D C: United States Office of Education, 1966.

SKINNER, B. F. *Beyond Freedom and Dignity.* New York: Bantam Books, 1971.

———. *Science and Human Behavior.* New York: Macmillan, 1953.

THORNDIKE, EDWARD L. *Animal Intelligence.* New York: Macmillian, 1911.

WATSON, JOHN B. *Behaviorism.* Revised ed. New York: Norton and Company, 1930.

———. "Psychology as the Behaviorist Views It." In *Psychological Review* 20 (1913): 158–177; reprint, *Psychological Review* 101 (1994): 248–253.

WIENER, NORBERT. *Cybernetics.* 2d ed. Cambridge: M. I. T. Press, 1961.

———. *The Human Use of Human Beings.* Boston: Houghton Mifflin, 1954; reprint, The Da Capo Series in Science. New York: Da Capo Press, 1988.

5

Music Teaching

INTRODUCTION AND OBJECTIVES

Much of what is known about learning is speculative, but research studies, historical data, and insight acquired from students confirm that learning is easier and more efficient when teachers do certain things or when they do *not* do certain things. This chapter focuses on teacher actions and decisions as they affect learning. It discusses the teacher's primary responsibility: that of structuring environments and classroom situations so that learning is more likely to occur. Some ideas and techniques presented here are especially pertinent to music instruction, but many others are equally appropriate for any discipline.

Studying Chapter 5 will enable readers to do the following:

- Explain the teacher's role in the classroom.
- List and describe at least two types of expository and interactive teaching.
- Describe the manner in which expository and interactive teaching affect the learning environment.
- Explain the difference between instructional goals or objectives and behavioral goals or objectives.
- Name and describe at least three types of student evaluation commonly used in music classes and give examples of situations in which each would be most appropriate.
- Outline the primary characteristics of pedagogical approaches described at the end of the chapter and discuss them as they relate to information presented in this and the two preceding chapters.
- Plan a lesson designed to help students acquire basic musical knowledge or skills.

PREPARATION FOR TEACHING

Teachers often begin by planning what they will do or what experiences they will use in the classroom rather than by deciding what students must learn and what they, as teachers, must do to help them. Concentrating on teacher behaviors (lecturing, assigning, conducting, or testing) or musical experiences (listening, singing, playing instruments) rather than on student learning confuses means with ends, however. When used in music classrooms, lecturing, conducting, singing, and playing instruments are processes through which teachers hope to bring learning about, but research suggests that teaching is most effective and efficient when its outcome is specified in advance. Thus, effective teaching begins with effective planning in which classroom situations are designed to encourage some predetermined learning. Classroom activities are thereby more successful because careful, goal-directed planning ensures that subject matter, student behaviors, instructional materials, and teacher actions are relevant and appropriate.

Inasmuch as learning is acquired and demonstrated through some type of behavior, planning for teaching focuses on student and teacher actions. Two kinds of content-behavior linkages must be established. The first is *instructional:* how students will get or learn information and how teachers can determine which student and teacher behaviors are most appropriate for bringing about the desired outcome. The second content-behavior linkage is *evaluative* or *behavioral:* how students will show what they have learned and how teachers can determine the effectiveness of the instructional behaviors they have selected and utilized.

Instructional Goals and Objectives

Instructional goals and objectives state what teachers want students to learn. These statements are general or specific, depending on whether they are for all students or for a particular class, small group, or ensemble. The level of specificity determines whether these statements are goals or objectives. To say, for instance, that students will learn about ternary form (content) is to make a general statement about desired outcomes. Such an *instructional goal* statement might be found in curriculum resources developed for general use. For instructional effectiveness in specific classroom settings, however, teachers must go farther. They must decide exactly what students should know about ternary form. Students may learn that ternary form has three sections, that it depends on a specific arrangement of repeated and contrasting sections, that it is used frequently in musical composition, or any combination of these. The point is that each of these is more precise than the instructional goal statement. These are in fact *instructional objectives* because they identify specific aspects or characteristics of the subject matter.

Sequencing Goals and Objectives

Once appropriate instructional objectives have been determined, they must be put in some kind of order. Experiences must be appropriate for the students' current maturity and ability levels. In other words, teachers must begin where students are and move forward. At the same time, because some ways of using newly acquired knowledge are more difficult than others, educators must also be sure that what they ask students to do with new information is not too advanced or complex.

The simplest way to determine where instruction should begin and how students might reasonably be expected to use new information is to consider such things as (1) prerequisite concepts and competencies required by the desired learning, (2) where students are now in relationship to these prerequisites, (3) what they will have to do or know in order to progress from where they are toward the desired learning, and (4) what kinds of experiences will facilitate this forward movement. Information about learning and development (see Chapter 3) and the taxonomies presented in Chapter 4 assist teachers in making these determinations. As a general rule, however, it helps to remember that learning is most effective when it progresses from the known to the unknown, from easy to difficult, from simple to complex, from concrete to abstract, from obvious to subtle, and in the case of skills, from crudeness to precision, from dependence to independence, and from application to creation.

Determining and sequencing instructional goals and objectives are the first steps when preparing for teaching, but planning that ends here usually emphasizes what teachers will do without indicating with any degree of clarity how students will acquire knowledge and skills. To be effective, teachers must go beyond sequencing content and determine the means by which students are most likely to learn the content. Teachers must decide on the best way of helping students acquire the desired knowledge, then plan activities that allow students to interact with subject matter in order to internalize knowledge and skills. Stated another way, effective educators develop lesson strategies that describe actual musical experiences—the music activities through which they will help students acquire the desired music learning.

Learning experiences encompass everything that teachers help students do with music in order to achieve the instructional objectives (and by extension, the instructional goals). Lesson plans are descriptions of these experiences. They tell exactly what will occur over time as teachers move students from where they are toward the desired outcome. Clear statements about specific observable and incremental aspects of learning are the essence of successful planning. Because people learn in a variety of ways, learning experiences must utilize several pedagogical approaches. The following section summarizes some of these.

SELECTING LEARNING EXPERIENCES

General Instructional Strategies

Expository Methods

All forms of expository teaching are teacher dominated and involve giving students information directly. Lecturing, the purest form of expository teaching, is used extensively at most levels of schooling. Lectures are usually highly structured aural presentations that are effective for dispensing verbal information such as facts, terms, descriptions, defini-tions, and principles to a large group. They are usually one-way modes of presentation, with information flowing from the teacher to the students, and they afford little opportu-nity for teachers to interact with students or for students to interact with one another and with musical materials. Outlines, study guides, work sheets, summaries, and question-and-answer periods may be used to generate some student activity and involvement, but this form of teaching is insufficient for most learning situations because it focuses more on what the teacher does to teach than on what students must do to learn.

Deductive teaching is another kind of expository instruction. Teachers present gen-eralizations or rules (and perhaps provide several samples or illustrations) from which stu-dents deduce other, more specific examples. For instance, the teacher presents the rule for constructing major triads and gives several examples of building major triads according to this rule. Students then build several more triads using the rule. Research suggests that teaching with rules may be more effective than any other teaching approach if speed and retention of learning are of particular concern.

Demonstrating or modeling is an effective and widely used expository technique, es-pecially for teaching musical skills. Teachers present an example of what is to be learned (a live demonstration, a picture or videotaped model, an audio recording, a verbal expla-nation), and students imitate it. Much music teaching in performance groups and applied lessons consists of modeling. For optimal learning to take place, students should be al-lowed to execute trial performances and receive feedback, which helps them refine the skill or behavior. This performance-oriented approach to teaching is a natural avenue for active learning.

Interactive Teaching Methods

Interactive teaching differs from expository instruction in that students learn by do-ing, even in the initial presentation of information. Rather than being a teacher-centered method in which learners remain relatively passive, interactive teaching (even in large-group situations) makes each learner a participant in the presentation. These methods in-volve exchanges between the teacher and students, students and their peers, instructional materials and students, and any combination of these. Interactive teaching thus includes various configurations of discussion, discovery, and problem-solving activities.

Since individuals, not ensembles, learn, behavior is elicited from each learner (even in bands, orchestras, and choirs), and teaching methods are deemed effective when each student actually attains the instructional objective. In many interactive methods, learners assume a large measure of control over their own materials, sequencing, and evaluation and may even help to establish instructional objectives for a class period or unit.

The most obvious alternative to the lecture is discussion, through which one-way teacher-student communication is expanded to include pupil-to-teacher and pupil-to-pupil communication. Discussions may be structured in one of three ways. First, they may be entirely pupil centered so that students freely exchange ideas, viewpoints, opinions, or feelings without much conscious regard for prescribed instructional objectives. In this situation, the teacher restates and helps to clarify students' ideas. This encounter-group approach is particularly useful when the instructional objective focuses on affective learnings such as musical preferences and value judgments. As these sessions become more teacher dominated (as when old-fashioned recitation is used), they become highly structured question-answer settings, relying on rote teaching and drill for achieving objectives. In essence, they become lectures.

It would seem that an approach between the two extremes would be appropriate for most classroom settings. In directed discussions, skilled teachers never lose sight of predetermined instructional objectives and continually steer exchanges toward them. As moderators, they hold students on track reasonably well (without dominating the discussion or simply dispensing information) while allowing students to express their ideas. Care must be taken that discussions are not monopolized by a few verbally adept students, however. This creates a lecture-type situation with added liabilities. When students do not have sufficient background in the content being discussed, or if a few individuals expound excessively on their narrow biases, discussions become counterproductive and degenerate into very quiet periods.

Discovery teaching can be placed on a continuum from exposition (in which all information is given by the teacher) to unguided discovery (in which students gather data, formulate concepts or principles, and solve problems more or less by themselves). Thus, the discovery or problem-solving instructional method can provide another major contrast with expository teaching. For situations or problem-solving tasks in which there is one "correct" answer, discovery teaching is an inductive approach in which students move from specific observations to rules. (Note that this is the opposite of the deductive approach discussed earlier.) Teachers present concrete examples and illustrations and let students unearth the underlying concepts and principles that support them.

On the other hand, there may be many correct answers or solutions for activities in which problem-solving instruction is appropriate because these situations usually require higher level open-ended induction. Composing music is one such task; there is no single correct answer here as there typically is in theory exercises. Composing, then, affords opportunities to experiment and take risks—if the teacher allows for it. This and other problem-solving tasks also allow students to assume more responsibility for their learning. For instance, students may be asked to take their choice of rhythm instruments into an adjoining room and create a short rhythm composition (meeting specific criteria), which they subsequently perform for the class. This type of learning experience is a good way to individualize learning and encourage creative use or application of knowledge and skills.

Specific Teaching Strategies

Facilitating Conceptual Development

A concept is generally defined as an idea or understanding, especially one derived from specific experiences. In a more technical sense, however, a concept is a category or classification of phenomena. Developing or acquiring concepts involves discriminating to determine which examples belong to a certain category and which ones do not. Later, generalizations are based on this concept—on characteristics of things belonging to this class or category. For example, everyone who knows what a chair is has a concept of "chairness." When a new or unfamiliar object is encountered, it is analyzed according to attributes that define "chairs," and one is able to determine whether the new object belongs to the "chair" category or class of phenomena.

Musical characteristics are categorized and labeled similarly. For students to understand concepts about melody, harmony, rhythm, form, and texture, teachers must take them beyond mere definitions. Definitions are useful starting places, but they are only partial concepts (or partial descriptors of a class or category). Consider the concept *staccato*. Beginning music students often learn that it means *short*, but after repeated contact with the concept, they gain a clearer and deeper understanding. They gradually understand that because the relative length of separated tones is regulated by such factors as tempo, dynamic levels, and historical style, the appropriate separation in the context of a specific musical passage dictates the interpretation of the staccato style. Over time and as the result of repeated experiences with the use of staccato in many contexts, students realize that spacing, not shortness, is the critical controlling factor.

Box 5–1 outlines a strategy for teaching concepts. Each of the five components is important. It is beneficial for students to experience concepts on a subconscious level before they are named or before students are made aware of what they are actually doing. Later, when concepts included in the activities are discussed and named and students become aware of them, the names, symbols, and meanings are more likely to be remembered because students will associate them with experiences (a song, a dance, a recording, a sound, a feeling). In addition, research suggests that concepts are learned more effectively when teachers provide both positive examples or referents (instances of the musical phenomenon) and negative examples (instances of what the musical phenomenon is not). Students then learn to identify critical attributes without being influenced by irrelevant ones.

BOX 5–1   A Strategy for Teaching Concepts

Concepts are ideas or categories of phenomena. The student must discriminate, classify, and apply them to learn them.

1. Present referents (concrete if possible, not verbal substitutes). Demonstrate, describe, explain, and/or illustrate the critical attributes. Help students see/hear what they might otherwise miss.
2. Present other examples and nonexamples to discriminate.
3. Have students practice applying concept. Behavioral objectives state how a concept is to be processed or used.
4. Provide knowledge of progress, confirmation, feedback.
5. Label and possibly define.

Facilitating Psychomotor Learning

The preceding discussion focused on cognitive learning, but most music programs emphasize technique and performance skills. As was mentioned, the demonstration method (or modeling) is most effective for helping students develop these kinds of skills. Imitation is probably the primary stimulus for all early learning. Young children imitate their parents while acquiring speech and are reinforced for appropriate discriminations. They imitate their peers and sometimes their teachers. When used in formal instruction, this process consists of three steps: (1) teacher modeling or presentation, (2) student practice or imitation, and (3) teacher feedback or evaluation. (See Box 5–2.)

First, the teacher presents the skill through demonstration, explanation, information, illustration, or any combination of these. This presentation clarifies the instructional objective for the activity and enables students to learn the skill more efficiently. Next, the learners practice the skill. Early attempts to execute it may be crude. Teachers "shape" the learners' behavior by accepting their initial gross approximations, then gradually helping them refine their performance until the desired standard is met. This does not mean that learners should be allowed to practice mistakes, however. Their attempts are guided by the performance standard established during the teacher's presentation, and they are encouraged to focus on and practice specific movement problems in order to correct them. Ini-

---

BOX 5–2   Demonstration (Modeling) Method for Teaching Psychomotor Skills

Model
teacher
	Demonstrate (show what is to be learned)
	Present
	Explain
	    oral instructions
	    written instructions
	Illustrate
	    charts, diagrams, pictures, films, recordings

Practice
student
	Imitate the Model
	Drill
	Learner trials guided by goal (model)
	    silent practice
	    spaced practice
	    drill on problems out of context

Evaluate teacher and student	**Feedback/Confirmation** Knowledge of results Proprioceptive stimulation muscle/visceral feel Knowledge of progress Self-criticism

tially, teachers provide feedback, but students must also learn to evaluate themselves in order to modify and improve their performance as they practice.

Studies show that practice is most beneficial if spaced over time and if learners are taught how to practice. With the teacher's help, they learn to alternate short but frequent rest periods with focused, concentrated practice periods. Students should also be taught to practice silently, actually fingering their instruments or thinking through their music while waiting to perform. This type of individualized practice can easily be developed and used in group situations.

Learning from a model demonstration depends on establishing bonds among the guiding model, students' kinesthetic responses, and such external stimuli as musical notation or conducting gestures so that eventually the external stimuli are enough to elicit appropriate responses. Students who are encouraged to note how movements or articulations "feel" when they execute them will become attuned to the kinesthetic responses or internal physical states accompanying various movements. This *proprioceptive feedback* is the body's way of helping a student learn physical or muscular skills.[1]

Also, when students are having difficulty with certain movements, direct physical guidance and "fading" techniques may be used. For example, string teachers may physically bow with beginning students, gradually releasing their grip on the bow until these students are bowing in the desired manner by themselves. Even at higher academic levels (in conducting classes, for instance) instructors may physically hold the baton along with the neophyte to guide him or her through difficult conducting problems such as fermati.

Demonstration or modeling also works well in ensemble rehearsals, expanded to include three subordinate components: synthesis-analysis-synthesis (whole-part-whole). First, the ensemble plays or sings through as much of a new composition as appropriate so that the students get a sense of how it goes. Meanwhile teachers listen, detect errors, and pinpoint problems related to technique, balance, style, intonation, and so forth. This comprises the first whole, or *synthesis*. The *analysis* phase consists of a three-step procedure similar to the one for modeling. (See Box 5–3.) Teachers provide models to show what the correct version looks or sounds like. A student whose performance approximates the model may also be asked to demonstrate correct rhythm, articulation, style, tone, or whatever needs correction. After students have established an aural or visual concept of the "correct" performance, they are given an opportunity to practice it. After the analysis phase, in the second *synthesis* phase, students perform the composition again in its entirety to demonstrate the results of their hard work and to provide a sense of fulfillment and closure for the day's rehearsal. Teachers provide positive and constructive feedback about this performance and plan to repeat the entire synthesis-analysis-systhesis cycle during the next rehearsal for continued refinement.

---

[1] *Proprioceptive* refers to sensations that occur within an organism as a result of movements of its own tissues. One example of a proprioceptive response is muscle feel. This feel is manifest in such musical behavior as singing or playing an instrument while reading music. Proprioceptive stimuli mediate rhythmic/metric timing and motor skills for performance. They are closely allied with the affective performance behavior discussed in the next section.

BOX 5–3   Demonstration Model for Ensemble Rehearsals

SYNTHESIS I   Ensemble plays composition through; teacher/conductor listens for problem spots and errors.

ANALYSIS   1. Teacher or student demonstrates (shows what is correct, e.g., rhythm, notes, style, balance, technique, articulation, intonation, dynamics, phrasing) by counting, singing, clapping, chanting, or playing.
Explain what a correct performance should look or sound like if you cannot demonstrate.
2. Emphasize important aspects of the correct performance by describing them or asking questions that help students identify them.
3. Have ensemble, section, or individual play, sing, or clap the parts of the composition that need correction.
Practice technical problems at a slow tempo. Practice rhythm problems on one note or have students count as they clap or tap the pattern.

SYNTHESIS II   Ensemble plays the composition again; teacher/conductor listens.
Teacher/conductor tells the ensemble what is
1. Good—Acceptable
2. Needs improvement
Plan to review during the next rehearsal if this performance shows little improvement over the one in Synthesis I.

Facilitating Affective Learning

Affective learning includes such outcomes as attitudes, preferences, values, and aesthetic sensitivity. Cognitive and motor-skill objectives equip students to perform. Affective learning determines whether students *will* perform under appropriate conditions. Because affective outcomes do not exist in isolation from cognitive and psychomotor learnings, many authorities argue against separating one kind of learning from another. They point out that affective learning is an inevitable by-product of other learning situations. Students not only learn content and skills but, in the process, to like or dislike the subject. There is always interaction among thinking, doing, and feeling. This argument notwithstanding, attitudes, preferences, and the like have a direct bearing on learning. In some ways how something is taught is more important to students' attitudes than what is taught. This is reason enough for teachers to be attuned to this aspect of learning.

Attitudes are positive or negative predispositions of varying intensity toward music or musical situations and may be inferred from students' behavior. These predispositions can usually be described in terms of seeking or avoiding tendencies: students who enjoy music classes want to attend those classes and are more likely to learn from them. Teachers must promote this level of interest.

Positive attitudes toward a subject usually result from positive, pleasant experiences with it. Teacher behaviors that make learning enjoyable help to foster positive attitudes. Such behaviors include clarifying objectives and presenting a rationale for learning tasks and experiences; motivating students to achieve by establishing realistic expectations and ensuring their success; and providing frequent and positive reinforcement and feedback.

Shaping students' musical preferences is a closely related problem. Although music teachers must not tell students what to like, as musical leaders in the community they do provide models of musical taste. Since respected and admired teachers—in short, effective teachers—are often emulated (with or without their knowledge), their actions and attitudes potentially have considerable influence.

The aesthetic dimension of affective behavior is developed through proprioceptive response. A common-sense expression sometimes used in skill learning is that students are "trying to get the feel of it." Similarly, educators help students get the expressive "feel" of music. In this way, the aesthetic or emotive aspects of musical performance are developed. Performers are often instructed to play with "feeling." This does not mean that they should project personal feelings into music, but rather that their responses to music should be emotive—in the sense of motion or kinesthesis, as discussed in Chapter 2. This motion is in the music and is conveyed in the score when it is read and interpreted musically. Students learn to recognize tonal tendencies, phrase movement and melodic contour, unexpected turns of phrase, rhythmic drives, stress and restraint, and harmonic movement from tension to cadential repose. Because these are associated with and remembered as muscular and visceral tensions (proprioceptive stimuli), students "feel" the music as they peform it, which comes through in their performances as musical expression.

Teachers facilitate development of this sensitivity by systematically emphasizing the expressive structure of music. They may select an instructional objective such as "The student will respond to the phrasing and 'line' of music." This objective would be realized through activities that incorporate performing, moving, listening, and creating, such as the following:

1. Students mark phrases in the music they are performing.
2. Students sing or play phrases while (a) physically moving, to show progression from the beginning of the phrase to the cadence, (b) using dynamic shading to underscore phrase shape by getting louder toward the middle of the phrase and softer toward the end, and (c) using rubato to help underscore the shape of the phrase.
3. Students indicate the "feeling" of phrases through movement and with diagrams or score markings.
4. Students select the "best" performance of a phrase and give reasons for their choice.
5. Students improvise phrases using techniques from item 2.
6. Students compose phrases and notate them, including expressive markings to underscore phrase shape and "feel."

ASSESSING TEACHING AND LEARNING

Formulating Behavioral Objectives

Behavioral goals (or *behavioral objectives*), the second type of content-behavior linkage mentioned earlier in this chapter, are more concerned with actual outcomes of instruction, whereas instructional goals and objectives focus on how students acquire knowledge and skills. For instance, behavioral goals tell what students will do after gathering new data about ternary form to demonstrate that they have learned this specific aspect of ternary form. Descriptions of behaviors to demonstrate that learning has occurred also explain how students will be affected by the new learning—how their behavior will be different because of specific classroom experiences. In short, these linkages allow teachers to determine what students have actually learned.

Well-formulated behavioral objectives consist of five parts: (1) a description of the learner, (2) an observable, measurable behavior, (3) specific content or subject matter, (4) the conditions under which new or modified behaviors (learning) will be demonstrated, and (5) specific standards or criteria to be used when assessing these behaviors. (See Figures 5–1 and 5–2.)

The *learner description* specifies the group of students to which the objective applies. Any clear and accurate description of students is appropriate. Thus, statements such as "general music students," "chorus members," or "band members" are all acceptable learner descriptions. Clearly, the more specific these descriptions are, the better they are because they reveal more information about the specific learners involved.

FIGURE 5–1   Behavioral objectives (goals).   *Source:* Adapted from Joseph A. Labuta, *Guide to Accountability in Music Instruction* (West Nyack, NY: Parker Publishing Company, 1974; copyright assigned to Joseph A. Labuta, 1991), 44.

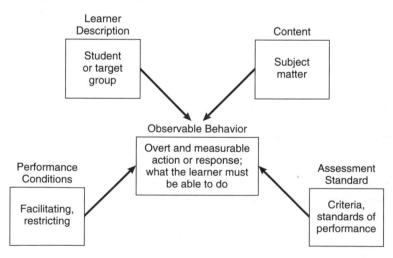

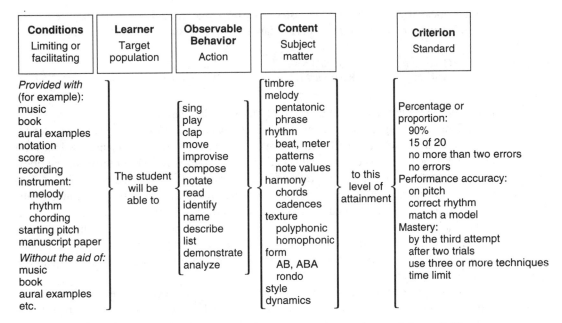

FIGURE 5–2 Musical objectives chart. *Source:* Adapted from Joseph A. Labuta, *Guide to Accountability in Music Instruction* (West Nyack, NY: Parker Publishing Company, 1974; copyright assigned to Joseph A. Labuta, 1991), 46.

In behavioral objectives, *overt behaviors,* that is, observable and measurable actions or products of an action, are described rather than covert or internal states of mind or feeling. As previously stated, covert changes must be inferred from overt behavior. To "love" music, "appreciate" it, "know" about it, and "really understand" it are goals that have merit, but given their covert (or internal) nature, they are impossible to assess. Instead, teachers must use overt indicators of covert understanding, knowledge, appreciation, and the like, as demonstrated in the following example:

> Students will demonstrate understanding of musical styles by correctly identifying in writing nine out of ten recorded examples played by the instructor as being from the Renaissance through Contemporary periods.

The *content* component of behavioral objectives refers to subject matter—in the preceding example, to musical styles. The content might just as easily have been musical forms, with fugue, binary, and theme and variations forms offered as choices. The critical factor to note is that this component must include some type of *musical* knowledge or skill that students have learned.

Well-constructed objectives specify the limiting or facilitating *conditions* under which students will perform. These may include a description of the materials, equipment, or other aids they may use, or the restrictions imposed on students' performances at the time of evaluation. Indications of performance conditions include the following:

Given . . .	Provided with . . .	With the aid of . . .
Without . . .	Restricted from . . .	Without the aid of . . .

Performance conditions should be relevant but not redundant or trivial.

The final component of behavioral objectives is the *performance standard* or criterion, which describes how well learners are expected to perform and to what level they are expected to achieve. Criteria can be stated in a variety of ways: (1) in terms of the number, percentage, or proportion of test items to be answered or executed correctly (e.g., no more than two errors, or 90 percent correct), (2) in terms of time limit (e.g., within ten minutes, (3) in terms of performance accuracy, skill criteria, or correspondence to a model (e.g., singing in tune, maintaining a steady beat, or performing correct rhythm patterns), and (4) in terms of mastery (e.g., achieve by the third attempt, or using all of the principles). Criteria or performance standards may be omitted if test items clarifying them are included in the objective.

When properly used, behavioral objectives constitute formative evaluation. Bloom and others advocate using this form of assessment, which is designed as an integral, ongoing part of the teaching and learning process. (The opposite of this, summative evaluation, is used as an end-of-the-course or terminal assessment, to determine grades.) Evaluation during the music program serves a larger purpose than assigning marks at the end of the semester. Continuous and comprehensive evaluation is essential because results are used to improve instruction. They make teachers aware of students' strengths and weaknesses and provide the information and guidance necessary for student improvement. More important, evaluation ascertains the extent of student learning and helps to determine the effectiveness of teaching. In these ways, everyone benefits from frequent and appropriate evaluation.

Objective-Referenced Tests

With clearly stated objectives in hand, teachers may develop additional evaluation instruments for measuring their attainment. Classifying objectives according to type or domain is an important first step in selecting or developing appropriate evaluation methods. As described in Chapter 4, objectives used in the music curriculum are classified in one of four categories: (1) verbal/cognitive, (2) aural/cognitive, (3) psychomotor, and (4) affective. Each area suggests appropriate modes of testing, but a frequently used assessment strategy, regardless of the domain, is the *objective-referenced* test, which consists of specific tasks or items serving as evidence of student learning. It measures the extent to which an individual has reached the instructional goal.

When developing these tests, the teacher must envision exactly what students should be doing when successfully achieving an objective so that test items engage them in the same performance that the behavioral objective prescribes. Testing need not be limited to

pencil and paper activities; playing, singing, and demonstrating can all be formal test behaviors. Testing may also be informal. Talking with students and asking questions or observing their current performance level are acceptable modes of assessment.

Measuring Verbal/Cognitive Learning

Knowledge and the cognitive processes associated with it include objectives related
to recognizing, recalling, and classifying such things as musical symbols (notation), musical vocabulary, and information about musical elements, form, historical periods, composers, and musical functions. Knowledge (especially the most basic type, which is
memory or recall) is easily tested in a group situation. Assessing knowledge requires verbal
or symbolic responses. Any pencil-and-paper, objective test format such as true-false,
multiple-choice, matching, and fill-in-the-blank, is applicable. The multiple-choice format
is especially useful because it is objective and easy to grade. Some teachers prefer short-
answer or essay questions, however, because these determine what students recall rather
than what they recognize. Because it is easy to test for information, formal assessment of
knowledge objectives is usually overdone. Note that the lowest-level and least important
music objectives (i.e., recognizing, recalling, and classifying) tend to fall in the category.
(See Box 5–4.)

Assessing Aural/Cognitive Learning

Perceptual awareness of music requires applying knowledge and classifying musical stimuli. It combines musical perception with cognitive processing to classify musical
elements, forms, historical styles, composers, and so forth. Listening tests, then, require an
appropriate aural stimulus (usually a recorded example) together with a pencil-and-paper
test. Such tests may include recognizing musical instruments by sound; taking melodic,
harmonic, or rhythmic dictation aurally; recognizing historical styles; and categorizing
musical examples on the basis of their texture. Because it is easy to generate test items for
aural perception objectives, mastery of these skills is easy to assess. Music listening tests
in general music, music appreciation, and music literature classes provide good examples
of this. (See Box 5–5.)

BOX 5–4 Measuring Verbal/Cognitive Learning

Objectives are related to:
 Recognizing, recalling, and classifying musical symbols, vocabulary, and information

Testing Format:
 Use paper-pencil format: multiple choice, true-false, completion, matching, essay
 questions

BOX 5–5   Assessing Aural/Cognitive Learning

Objectives are related to:
 Applying knowledge and classifying musical stimuli by listening to music

Testing Format:
 Use of aural stimulus and paper-and-pencil test.

Evaluating Psychomotor Achievement

Motor performance requires applying knowledge through physical response. This category of objectives must be evaluated through individual testing of singing, playing instruments, and reading music. Informal observations with a rating scale or checklist of performance behaviors are also helpful. (Adjudicator forms for solo and ensemble festivals provide a good example.) Audio- and videotape recordings may also be used extensively for evaluating skill in vocal and instrumental performance and in conducting. (See Box 5–6.)

Because evaluating individual performance skills in a large-group setting is difficult and time consuming, these tests must be approached in creative and novel ways. For example, an audiocassette tape recorder can be used to assess achievement of prescribed materials. During a full rehearsal, students go one at a time to an adjacent practice room and record their performance. Tapes can be evaluated later, during the conductor's free period, on a lunch hour, or at home.

Measuring Affective Learning

Affective learning is among the most important outcomes of music education, but music teachers tend to neglect these learnings because they are among the most difficult to assess. The affective domain includes musical preferences, attitudes toward music and mu-

---

BOX 5–6   Evaluating Psychomotor Achievement

Objectives are related to:
 Applying knowledge through physical response, such as playing, singing, and reading music

Testing Format:
 Use informal or formal observation utilizing rating scale, checklist, log, VCR, audiotape, etc.

BOX 5–7 Measuring Affective Learning/Development

Objectives are related to:
  Discerning preferences, positive attitude, aesthetic sensitivity (likes, dislikes, and feelings)

Testing Format:
  Use informal observation or systematic survey with checklist, daily log, anecdotal records, formal records—any nonreactive observational techniques

---

sic classes, and aesthetic sensitivity. Evaluating affective objectives remains a largely subjective operation, but Box 5–7 provides some guidelines.

Attitudes toward music classes can be assessed through systematic surveys involving students, classroom teachers, and parents. One can construct observation and survey instruments using approach and avoidance behaviors as indicators: Students' eagerness to come to music class offers valuable insight, for example. Survey items can be developed that can be answered with a yes or no, or can be rated on an intensity scale. This can be supplemented with a daily log in which anecdotal observations and comments about students are recorded. One affective outcome for which most music teachers strive is that students enjoy (like, prize, or love) their music classes. The following outline may be used as the basis of an attitudinal survey designed to obtain information from students, teachers, and parents.

Collecting Feedback from Students

Observing students informally or using a checklist may help to determine their attitudes toward music and music classes. All of the following items will not apply to every student, but a composite of items will indicate the direction of students' feelings. Find out if students do the following:

1. Elect music classes and musical activities when they have other alternatives
2. Regularly attend all classes, performances, and extra rehearsals
3. Participate in extra musical activities such as ensembles, solos, festivals, honors ensembles, all-city ensembles, and the like
4. Initiate musical activities
5. Do extra work for music class voluntarily
6. Arrange their schedules to accommodate musical activities
7. Seek help in musical endeavors
8. Voluntarily attend concerts and other musical programs
9. Help or work in the music room
10. Stay around the music room after rehearsal, after school, during free hours, and so forth

Getting Feedback from Classroom Teachers

Teachers often volunteer positive and negative information about their students' responses to music classes, but the following items help to survey students' attitudes about music more systematically. Ask teachers whether students

1. Want to go to music classes
2. Eagerly anticipate music classes
3. Talk enthusiastically about music class
4. Inform them about musical activities
5. Want to continue or initiate musical activities after returning to the regular classroom
6. Want to perform for the class
7. Talk to their peers about joining music classes, ensembles, other activities

Obtaining Feedback from Parents

As a general rule, parents only report extreme reactions to some aspect of the music program, such as high praise or adamant disagreement. A parent survey may elicit more objective data to use for student evaluation. Ask parents if students

1. Talk enthusiastically about their school music classes
2. Talk about musical programs, concerts, activities
3. Sing songs learned in school
4. Practice instruments or vocal parts voluntarily
5. Take private lessons
6. Participate in out-of-school musical activities such as a church choir or community instrumental ensemble
7. Voluntarily attend concerts and other musical activities outside of school
8. Listen to recordings—what kinds
9. Read books about music and musicians as a leisure activity
10. Talk about music as a possible vocation

A TEACHING/LEARNING STRATEGY

In light of all information presented in this and the two preceding chapters, the basic format presented next provides a model lesson plan that can be used to prepare for teaching most cognitive objectives. Any of the preceding methods, perhaps in combination, may be used when appropriate. Well-formulated instructional and behavioral objectives often suggest the most efficient and effective means of attaining them (i.e., the activities in which to engage students). Obviously, any strategy will have to be adjusted to the specific objectives and group of students. The model lesson plan includes five steps: (1) Provide purpose—present and clarify objectives, (2) motivate, or secure and maintain attention and commitment to the objectives, (3) establish learning readiness by reviewing prerequisite learning, (4) provide situations and activities that lead to objectives, and (5) provide feedback on the student's performance. (See Box 5–8.)

Provide Purpose—Present and Clarify Objectives

Research studies indicate that learning is more efficient when students understand exactly what they are expected to do or know at the end of the instructional period. Teachers must help learners extract their own learning from classroom experiences. In addition, students must respond to (and interact with) the environment in order to learn, so they must know the intended outcome of this interaction. When students cannot find relationships between the activity in which they are engaged and the objectives, learning is usually minimal. For example, when music students sing in the chorus; play in the orchestra; study, drill, and write exercises in theory class; listen to lectures; take part in discussion; and take notes, they are interacting to some extent. But they need to know why they are interacting, and this is precisely stated in your instructional objectives. Moreover, if students know in advance what is expected of them at the end of the interaction, as stated in the behavioral objectives, they can assume greater responsibility for their own learning and can evaluate their own progress toward attaining the goal.

Here are a few suggestions: (1) Tell students exactly what they are to accomplish; (2) when appropriate, give them a written copy of the objectives, stated in language that they can understand on their own; (3) present sample test questions; (4) give students examples or models of the terminal project; and (5) question the group at appropriate intervals to make sure that all students recall and understand what they are trying to achieve.

BOX 5–8   A Teaching/Learning Strategy

1. Provide purpose
      Present and clarify objectives
      Describe what is to be learned
2. Motivate: Secure and maintain students' attention and commitment to objectives
3. Establish learning readiness: Review prerequisite learning
4. Provide situations and activities that lead to objectives
      Give needed information, demonstrations
      Use appropriate media
      Provide for practice
      Provide for sequence (simple to complex, concrete to abstract)
5. Provide feedback on performance
      Knowledge of results, confirmation

Motivate—Secure Attention and Commitment

Students must accept the lesson objectives and be willing to work toward attaining them. Without commitment, there is minimal participation and response; without participation and response, there is no learning. *Motivation* is the term most often used to describe students' commitment to the learning experience, and often, the manner in which activities are presented is the most important aspect of the lesson.

It helps to be creative when "selling" objectives to students. If appropriate, use novel, unexpected, even somewhat shocking techniques (within reason, of course) such as demonstrations, visuals, or guest artists. As a general rule, however, know that a teacher's sincere belief in the value of what is to be accomplished can inspire students who might otherwise remain detached and uninvolved. Enthusiasm is always contagious, but it must never be forced or trite.

Maintaining commitment to the objectives is largely a matter of success and reinforcement through feedback. Review objectives and the rationale for achieving them frequently. In addition, structure learning situations for students success. Success, like frustration, is self-generating; a little of either leads to more of the same.

Establish Learning Readiness

Determine whether students are prepared to tackle the proposed learning tasks. Remedial work may be necessary before beginning instruction toward planned goals. If students are ready, a careful review of information, concepts, or skills prior to starting will make learning easier in that it will enable students to recall and use previously learned information and skills in the immediate learning situation. A review of this type establishes *learning readiness* by focusing attention on relevant stimuli. It also provides cues or prompts to direct learning.

Provide Appropriate Situations and Activities

Once students know and are committed to the objectives of the lesson or activity, they must engage in the learning tasks and behavior that will lead to the objectives. Methods discussed earlier will help students attain desired outcomes. Use expository methods to give directions and information needed to initiate learning; use interactive methods to generate responses. Have other necessary materials available so that learners can practice what is to be learned. Remember that overt practice affords an observable indication of progress, even for primarily covert or thinking tasks.

Students must also spend time doing things that are relevant to the desired learning. Planned activities must lead directly to the stated objectives. This may require modifying procedures, techniques, pedagogies, music lessons, method books, and other published materials. Often these are not directed toward specified instructional objectives, and without these, activities are just something to do and rarely lead to the desired learning. Instead of following a method book line by line or lesson by lesson, select activities based on their relevance to attaining the stated objectives, and be sure that these are the things students practice and do. Such focused experiences will lead to learning.

Provide Feedback on Performance

While students are involved in doing activities to achieve objectives, they must be informed about how well they are doing if learning is to progress. *Computer-assisted instruction* programs (CAI) are excellent conduits for feedback, because they indicate the accuracy of each response immediately. Resourceful teachers who do not have computers in the classroom also find ways to provide this immediate appraisal of students' performances, although not as efficiently, perhaps, as a computer program. They can do this informally through questioning, observing performance, using audio or visual recording equipment, and encouraging students to evaluate themselves. An appropriate verbal or gestural response—a smile, a nod, a comment such as "Good job!"—works well. Teachers must also remember to acknowledge correct responses right away. But whether responses are correct or not, ignoring responses soon extinguishes them.

Earlier, reference was made to formative and summative evaluation and the notion that all testing must be an integral, functioning part of the instructional process. Many people regard testing as something outside of, or in addition to, instruction. When teachers give tests in order to give grades, testing becomes an end in itself. Of course some music teachers abdicate the role of music evaluation and assign grades using such criteria as regular attendance, punctuality, and service.

Formative tests reinforce correct responses, but more important, they diagnose learning difficulties. In addition to showing what students have not learned, they provide insight about aspects of instruction that need to be modified or improved. Formative tests should occur at regular intervals before end-of-semester grading to identify unmastered material or skills, but they should not be used for actual grading. If it is necessary to provide some type of written appraisal of students, comments such as *pass* to indicate mastery of objectives, and *more work needed* or *not yet* for objectives not yet attained allow the tests to remain nonthreatening while serving their diagnostic function. Such tests must also be short enough that they do not take an inordinate amount of time to administer. Flash cards with answers written on the back work well for formative testing, as do teacher-developed self-scoring tests to accompany texts, lessons, method books, or other instructional media. If answer sheets are folded and stapled to the test sheet, students are able to check their answers as soon as they are ready to do so, whether at home or at school. This option provides immediate feedback to facilitate efficient learning. Finally, students may check each other's papers or grade their own during class time.

With this chapter Part II has come full circle. The investigation of school music curricula in Chapter 3 weighed what subject matter and skills students should acquire in school music classes. Chapter 4 examined various theories about how people learn and attempted to relate these general theories to music learning. The first half of this chapter used information about curriculum and the learning process to determine how teachers might facilitate and assess learning.

In light of the discussions about curriculum, learning, and teaching, it seems appropriate next to exam several music pedagogies commonly used in American schools today—those developed by Emile Jaques-Dalcroze, Carl Orff, Zoltán Kodály, Shinichi Suzuki, and Edwin Gordon.[2] While providing general pedagogical information that all music educators should be cognizant of, these pedagogies present examples of ways in which a number of musicians and music educators have attempted to resolve problems that classroom teachers face each day. This brief examination of current music pedagogy is followed by a presentation of general principles derived from the information presented in Part II.

CURRENT MUSIC PEDAGOGY

Emile Jaques-Dalcroze and Eurhythmics

Emile Jaques-Dalcroze (1865–1950) was born in Vienna and lived there ten years before his family moved to Geneva. His mother, a Pestalozzian music teacher, and his father, a Swiss merchant, provided a rich musical home environment for young Emile and his sister, frequently taking them to concerts, plays, and operas. Both children demonstrated musical ability and began studying music at a young age. Jaques-Dalcroze studied at the Conservatory of Music and the College of Geneva prior to spending three years as a member of the Belles-Lettres Society, where he acted, sang, and began composing for the theater. At age twenty-nine he moved to Paris and was active in a theater group while studying composition with Léo Delibes and Gabriel Fauré. He later traveled to Vienna to study composition with Anton Bruckner and Robert Fuchs before returning to Geneva to join the faculty at the conservatory.

While teaching at the conservatory, Dalcroze became increasingly troubled by several problems with the music instruction of the day. First, it was compartmentalized so that music history, theory, and other aspects of the discipline never came together in a comprehensive way during a student's course of study. Furthermore, students tended to approach harmony, theory, and performance in much the same way that they approached academic subjects—as a set of rules to memorize and symbols to manipulate. Students were unable to "hear" their harmonic exercises, and because theoretical knowledge was not internalized their musical expression was often technically flawless but stilted and without sensitivity.

He also noted a discrepancy between students' musical performance and their spontaneous responses while listening to music. They were often unable to play music with

---

[2] Much of the information about Dalcroze, Orff, and Kodály used in this summary is taken from Beth Landis and Polly Carter, *The Eclectic Curriculum in American Music Education: Contributions of Dalcroze, Kodály, and Orff* (Washington, DC: Music Educators National Conference, 1972); Lois Choksy and others, *Teaching Music in the Twentieth Century* (Englewood Cliffs: Prentice Hall, Inc., 1986); and Stanley Sadie, ed., *The New Grove Dictionary of Music and Musicians* (London: Macmillan Publishers Ltd., 1980). Information about Suzuki is found in Michael L. Mark, *Contemporary Trends in Music Education,* 2d ed. (New York: Schirmer Books, 1986); and Evelyn Hermann, *Shinichi Suzuki: The Man and His Philosophy* (Athens, OH: Ability Development Associates, 1981).

rhythmic accuracy and a free and emotive style, yet they were entirely capable of emotive and rhythmically precise spontaneous movements while listening to music. These observations raised a number of important questions in Dalcroze's mind, and his answers ultimately became the foundation of rhythmic movement, a crucial aspect of his pedagogical approach.

Dalcroze reasoned that music begins, or is generated, when human emotion[3] is translated into musical motion. People *sense* or *feel* the dynamism of emotion in various parts of the body in the form of muscular tension and relaxation, and they convey or express this feeling to others through gestures, facial expressions, postures, and the like. Some of these modes of expression are reflexive and spontaneous; others are willed or intentional. Thus, human movement is the means by which inner feeling is translated into musical responsiveness and, consequently, the human body is the first musical instrument on which students should receive instruction. All else—singing, playing instruments, composing—should be an extension of this.

Of the three elements of music as Dalcroze perceived them—sound (a combination of pitch, tone quality, and dynamics), rhythm, and dynamics—the latter two are entirely dependent on movement in time and through space. This movement, in turn, correlates with our muscular system, enabling us to express all rhythmic and dynamic aspects of music physically. Furthermore, the intensity of our physical sensations vary concomitantly with variations in these characteristics in music.

Given the importance that Dalcroze placed on this *kinesthesia* (or kinesthetic sense), it is not surprising that kinesthesia became the basis of this pedagogy. Students explore all aspects of musical sound via immediate physical response. Thus they must learn to listen intently. Primary learner objectives of eurhythmic training are (1) developing attention, (2) converting this attention into concentration, (3) developing awareness of relationships among personal responses to music, other people's responses to music, and musical organization and events (i.e., repetition and contrast, melodic and rhythmic motives, melodic contour, changes in dynamics or *tempo*); (4) developing awareness of which modes of response are most appropriate in a given context, and (5) developing ability to respond to and express all nuances of sound and feeling. In addition, eurhythmics[4] aims to merge physical flexibility (easy and accurate movement and ability to express oneself through movement) with musical ability (increasingly discriminating responses to musical sound whether one is listening to, performing, analyzing, reading, writing, or creating music).

Once students acquire some facility with rhythmic movement, Dalcroze pedagogy seeks to help them internalize how movements feel, look, and sound. This *inner hearing* also develops kinesthetic imagination and memory as students accumulate a vocabulary of movements with their attendant sensations, sounds, and images. Students gradually internalize musical concepts as a result of experiencing them, and this internalization is as much physical and sensate as it is musical and emotive.

---

[3] The word *emotion* is used here in the broad sense, as discussed at length in Chapter 2. Dalcroze was concerned with the rhythmic or dynamic quality of all emotion or feeling rather than with the nature of specific emotions such as sadness and joy.

[4] Eurhythmics, the name given to this pedagogy, derives from its emphasis on rhythmic movement.

Jaques-Dalcroze's method has become known in the United States as eurhythmics or the movement pedagogy, but rhythmic movement is only one facet of this pedagogical approach. The second aspect is solfege, activities that involve pitch (i.e., voice and eartraining, reading musical scores, identifying intervals, and taking music dictation). Using the fixed-do system, students learn melodic and harmonic concepts in much the same way that they learn rhythmic ones: by associating movement with sound and by responding to sound physically. An additional goal of this instruction is to develop a strong sense of pitch memory so that by the end of extended Dalcroze training in solfege some students develop near-perfect relative pitch.

A beginning solfege activity might require, for instance, that children imagine themselves to be snowpeople, and as the teacher plays a descending melodic line, their bodies melt in the sun. Children might also walk as the teacher plays a melodic line, changing their direction as the teacher's melody changes direction and stepping in place when pitches are repeated. Later, children learn to step melodies using normal steps for whole steps and small or baby steps for melodic half steps.[5]

Harmonic activities are more complex. Beside distinguishing two or more melodic lines that are sounding simultaneously, children must coordinate their movements to music with those of other children. In a two-part texture, for example, one child moves according to the higher voice while another child moves with the lower one. When the two melodic lines are in unison, the two children's movements must be the same.[6] Students begin learning to improvise on instruments and with the voice from the beginning of instruction. The primary objective here is synthesis: to development skill in combining movement (rhythm), sound (pitch, harmony, phrasing, and so forth), and dynamics in imaginative, spontaneous, and personally expressive ways.

Dalcroze pedagogy first came to the attention of music educators in 1905 when it was demonstrated in Switzerland for an international audience of music educators. Since then this pedagogy, initially developed for conservatory students, has been used successfully with youngsters worldwide. In addition, Dalcroze's impact on the entire field of dance, on rhythmic theory, and on pedagogy in general attest to the importance of his ideas for music instruction and human expression.

Zoltán Kodály and Sol-Fa

Hungarian-born composer, ethnomusicologist, and educator Zoltán Kodály (1882–1967), like Dalcroze, was distressed by the state of music education in his homeland. In addition to the meager music literacy skills demonstrated by students entering the most advanced music education institution in Hungary, these students had no knowledge of their musical heritage. There were essentially two musical cultures in Hungary during the early 1900s. One was for the elite and educated and was centered on German and Viennese music. The other was for the common people and primarily included Hungarian folk music. Although

---

[5] Elsa Findley, *Rhythm and Movement: Applications of Dalcroze Eurhythmics* (Princeton, NJ: Summy–Birchard Music, 1971), 48–53.

[6] Ibid.

Kodály eventually studied at the Academy of Music while receiving instruction at Budapest University and was exposed to some classical music in his home as a child, he had spent the first years of his life among countryfolk whose musical activities were grounded in folk music. This made a lasting impression on him.

His interest in native Hungarian music developed such that the terminal project for his doctoral degree was an analytical thesis on folk song structure. As part of this study (completed in 1906) he gathered the first of thousands of folk tunes, marking the beginning of a lifelong effort to collect, analyze, classify, and popularize his country's music. Béla Bartok (1881–1945), a native Hungarian and one of the twentieth century's most influential composers, joined him in this project some years later. Between them, they had collected and classified 100,000 folk songs by the 1950s.

Kodály and Bartok shared the vision of a musically literate Hungary, but it was Kodály's philosophy, principles, and goals that evolved into the Hungarian way of music education. This philosophy included six primary points: (1) Everyone who is capable of developing language literacy is capable of becoming musically literate; (2) singing is the best and most natural, practical, and effective means of acquiring musicianship; (3) to be most effective, music education must begin when children are very young; (4) children's "mother tongue" should serve as the foundation of early instruction; (5) music teaching should use only repertoire of the highest quality; and (6) music should be a core subject in school curricula.

Initially, Kodály sought to increase music literacy in Hungary by improving teacher preparation courses. Although he made important inroads, significant changes in Hungarian music education did not occur until Marta Nemesszeghy, a longtime friend of Kodály, established and served as principal of the first Hungarian singing primary school. There, Kodály's ideas were set in motion and refined as children received daily music instruction.

The pedagogy known as the Kodály method, or "the singing method," stemmed from his ideas and philosophy. The sequential nature of its curriculum is largely of his design, but the instructional techniques used to attain the curriculum's musical objectives were borrowed from a variety of sources. The method by which students learn to read and write music under this curriculum is called *relative sol-fa* and was derived from the tonic sol-fa system developed and used in England by John Curwen sometime after 1840. This solfege method uses the movable- rather than fixed-do system, and pitches are represented by their initial letter (do becomes d, re becomes r, and so on).

For rhythmic notation Kodály deviated from Curwen's system, using stems without note heads except for half notes and notes of longer duration. To these he added rhythm syllables derived from French pedagogue Emile Chevè. He also adopted Curwen's hand signals, used for each pitch of the scale. (See Figure 5–3.) These signals were specifically designed to convey the tendencies of pitches as they are normally used in musical contexts. In addition, the method makes use of vertically arranged sol-fa syllables in a tonal or letter ladder, which was popularized by Sarah Glover, also in England. This ladder provides yet another visual representation of pitches and their relationships to other notes of the scale.

In addition to these tools, Kodály's pedagogical approach uses a number of other materials, all designed to accommodate young children's musical, mental, and physical

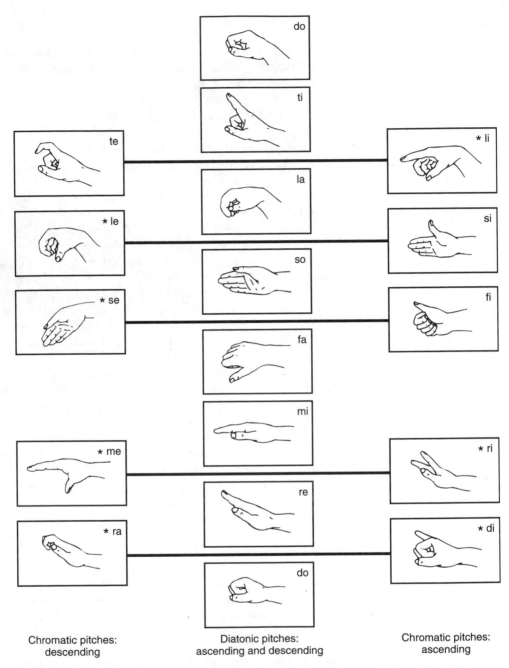

Chromatic pitches: descending	Diatonic pitches: ascending and descending	Chromatic pitches: ascending

FIGURE 5–3 Diatonic pitches: ascending and descending. *Source:* Adapted from Grant Newman, *Teaching Children Music* (Dubuque, IA: Wm. C. Brown Publishers, 1989), 317. Chromatic signals that are marked with an asterisk (signals for di, ri, li, ra, me, se, and le) were developed for this text by Deborah A. Smith so that each pitch in the chromatic scale has a corresponding hand signal.

needs. Use of the pentatonic (five-tone) scale, iconic notation (using figures other than traditional music symbols to represent aspects of music), musical games, and staff placemats
(sheets of paper or pieces of felt 8-1/2 × 11 inches or larger placed lengthwise, with five
lines representing the staff drawn on them) with markers or circular math counters for
notes are all based on Kodály's understanding of child development. Moreover, the entire
approach is developmental and sequential. As with Dalcroze eurhythmics, musical elements are experienced for some time at a subconscious level before notational symbols are
introduced. In addition, each element is thoroughly internalized in all of its most common
contexts before a new element is presented. Finally, Kodály composed hundreds of exercises and compositions at all levels of difficulty for use with this pedagogy.

Kodály lived to see the fruits of his ideas recognized internationally as well as in his
native Hungary, which actually became the musically literate country he had envisioned
so many years earlier. Following the method's initial presentation at the 1958 conference
of the International Society for Music Education (ISME) and similar presentations at two
subsequent ISME conferences, Kodály's homeland was flooded with visitors who observed the methodology firsthand and took the ideas back to their own education systems.

Carl Orff and Schulwerke

Like Dalcroze, German-born composer Carl Orff (1895–1982) did not set out to formulate
a general music pedagogy for young children. His involvement in music pedagogy was an
indirect result of his eclectic artistic interests in theater, folk music, ancient tragedy, and
Baroque music, among other areas. Also like Dalcroze, he began music study as a child
and continued those studies through graduation from the Munich Academy of Music in
1914.

The work that eventually led to development of *schulwerke* began in 1924 when he
and dancer Dorothee Günther established the Güntherschule in Munich. The primary objective of this establishment was to explore and teach new relationships between dance and
music that were becoming popular as part of a movement in dance known as "The New
Dance Wave." No doubt this revolution in dance was, at least in part, a result of Dalcroze's
influence, and Orff himself was similarly influenced by Dalcroze pedagogy.

Orff came to believe, perhaps as a result of eurhythmics, that rhythm was the most
important aspect of music, although he used the term rhythm in its more conventional
sense. Furthermore, his interest in "total theater" (as evidenced in his work *Carmina Bu-
rana* and developed in some of his other compositions and in his pedagogy) was an extension of this classical belief that music, movement, and speech were inseparable. The
concept became the basis for his *elemental music* or *recapitulation theory* of musical development.

Orff's theory asserts that each person's musical development progresses through
stages comparable to the development of music through history—from primal, rudimentary, rhythmic music making to the more sophisticated and refined music making of today.
Thus, the phrase *elemental music* refers to the starting point for musical development and
the manner in which people naturally express themselves through music at various stages
of development.

It is logical that Orff would advocate beginning music instruction with very young children and that teaching and learning should be active, participatory, and group oriented rather than receptive, soloistic, and static. With *schulwerke,* children's first experiences with formal music instruction involve games and playlike activities. They explore sounds, rhythms, and melodies and other musical elements in a rather informal way. The teacher, however, is consciously laying the foundation for subsequent study. During this period students are developing a working music vocabulary on which later music learning will be built. These initial experiences are entirely rote and involve a great deal of spontaneous music making. (Creativity is a prominent feature of Orff pedagogy at all levels.)

Rhythm, combined with speech and simple pentatonic melodies, is a logical starting place for instruction. These elements are combined with simple dances and other forms of basic movement. Moreover, the specially constructed instruments that have earned Orff's methodology the nickname *the instrument method* also developed as an extension of this elemental music theory. Orff's instruments include several varieties of melodic percussion instruments (glockenspiels, metallophones, and xylophones); timpani, hand drums, and other percussion instruments; recorders; and simple stringed instruments. These instruments provide another way for students to explore musical timbres while making music. Exploring these instruments and learning to use the singing voice musically and expressively precede the study of standard orchestral instruments. Orff instruments are ideally suited for the child's singing voice and for the musical activities that Orff believed were essential to optimal musical development. They are frequently used for improvisation (use of the pentatonic scale ensures that these spontaneous creativity sessions are errorproof), to provide simple *bordun* (drone) and *ostinato* (repetitive) accompaniments for rhythmic speech and singing, and for ensemble performances of children's songs.

These ideas were more systematized as a result of Orff's collaboration with Gunild Keetman, a former student at the Güntherschule. This partnership, which began in 1926, also led to publication of *Musik für Kinder* (Music for Children), a multi-volume set of materials designed specifically for use in Orff instruction, although they were initially designed for adult students. As is the case with the Dalcroze and Kodály pedagogies, Orff's approach to music education is entirely sequential and developmental. Only after students have acquired a working vocabulary of musical experiences are notational symbols introduced.

Shinichi Suzuki and Talent Education

The Suzuki pedagogical system became popular in this country during the 1960s when large groups of very young children were featured in demonstrations and presentations designed to disseminate the originator's ideas. The approach was initially developed for violin instruction, as Shinichi Suzuki was a violinist and came from a family of string performers and violin makers. Eventually he, along with his brother and sister-in-law, adapted the method for piano instruction.

Suzuki pedagogy is based on several notions. First, Suzuki believed that all children had the potential for excellence and that, in many instances, this potential remained undeveloped. In addition, he felt strongly, as did other pedagogues discussed here, that the critical years for talent development were the early childhood years—that formative period from birth to approximately age seven or eight when children begin acquiring many of the skills needed in adult life.

Next, he believed that musical perception and performance skills should be acquired in the same way that language skills are acquired: through repetition and rote memorization. Children should constantly be exposed to recorded and live examples of the highest level musical performance, and over time they would develop excellent aural skills. Similarly, when learning violin, children need the best teachers because they learn initially by imitating the teacher's model. Moreover, parental involvement is crucial to the success of music instruction, because parents are responsible for monitoring their children's daily practice at home and correcting technical and intellectual errors.

Suzuki's third principle, related to the second, is that just as children acquire the verbal language of their culture as their first experience with language, so their musical experience should begin with the music of their culture—their musical "mother tongue."

Edwin Gordon and Music Learning Theory

Edwin Gordon was born in 1927 and attended public schools in New York. Although there was little musical activity in his home, Gordon received music instruction at school. His memories of being classified a nonsinging "blackbird" by his fourth-grade teacher, and having to mouth the words and listen so that he might learn to sing, are vivid and frustrating even today.[7]

While studying string bass as a teenager, Gordon realized that, aside from being able to perform, he knew very little about music. Amidst this new frustration, Gordon began losing interest in studying music. Then, his teacher suggested that he study with Sid Weiss, the bass player who had played with Artie Shaw and was with Benny Goodman's band at that time. Lessons with Weiss lasted until Gordon's high school graduation in 1945 and marked a turning point in his musical training. More important, the improvisatory nature of these lessons established the foundation for the teaching and learning approach he formulated years later.

Immediately following graduation, Gordon was drafted into the army. Before long, he was playing in the 302 Army Band, an assignment requiring that he teach himself to play the tuba. While in the army band, Gordon spent his free time "jamming with the fine musicians in the band,"[8] and after being discharged from the army in 1947, he enrolled at Eastman School of Music in New York as a string bassist. Between 1947 and 1953 while Gordon was completing a bachelors and masters degree in string bass performance, he played with Gene Krupa's band in New York City, and shortly after Gordon's graduation from Eastman, he began private study with Philip Sklar, principal bassist of the NBC Symphony Orchestra. At Sklar's suggestion, Gordon enrolled at Ohio University in Athens,

[7] Edwin E. Gordon, "Gordon on Gordon," *The Quarterly* 2 (1991), 6–7.
[8] Ibid., 7.

Ohio, where he completed requirements for teacher certification and earned a second masters degree in music education.[9]

In 1958, Gordon completed doctoral studies at the University of Iowa, remaining there as a member of the faculty for fourteen years. Teaching music classes at the university and in the university's laboratory schools aroused his interest in the psychology of music, which he refers to as *music learning theory.* Gordon credits his studies with statistician Albert N. Hieronymous and his own familiarity with Carl E. Seashore's early twentieth-century investigations of musical psychology for his subsequent success with formulating the method of music instruction that many U.S. music educators are using today.[10]

Edwin Gordon's psychology of music learning, *music learning theory,* is the basis for his music method, which is also called music learning theory. The theory and method reflect general principles of educational psychology and focus on *audiation,* a term Gordon coined in 1976 for the ability to imagine musical sound when it is not present, and to make sense of musical sound while listening to, performing, creating, reading, and writing it.[11]

Audiation (or more specifically, the process by which this ability develops and is sustained) and music learning are synonymous. Gordon delineates seven types of audiation or stages of music learning: (1) listening to music, (2) reading music silently or while performing, (3) notating actual musical sound when taking music dictation, (4) recalling music silently or while performing, (5) notating music from memory, (6) improvising or creating music silently or while performing, and (7) notating improvised or created music. All of these types involve four audiational processes—listening, reading, recalling, and creating music—that are related to at least one of three kinds of musical activities: thinking about, writing, or performing music. Everyone has some ability to audiate or some aptitude for music learning, and the quality of one's musical involvement depends on a person's audiational facility. Consequently, developing this ability to audiate is of primary importance for music teachers.

Music learning theory is made up of stages that are hierarchically organized. The stages are not mutually exclusive because some behaviors associated with each of them occur concurrently with behaviors associated with others. Also, given Gordon's emphasis on audiation, it is not surprising that his music learning sequence is designed to develop and refine this ability. Audiation is the foundation of music understanding (comprehension) which is in turn the basis for aesthetic responses to music as discussed in Chapter 2 of this text. Since music is an aural art, music understanding requires that students have instinctive understanding of music's fundamental aural elements: tonality and meter. This musical understanding must be developed before students learn notation symbols or use technical language and terms to describe music. Though music literacy is the long-range

---

[9] Ibid., 8.

[10] Ibid.

[11] See Edwin Gordon, *Learning Sequences in Music: Skill, Content, and Patterns* (Chicago: G. I. A. Publications, 1980; reprint, Chicago: G. I. A. Publications, 1989); Darrel L. Waters and Cynthia Crump Taggart, *Readings in Music Learning Theory* (Chicago: G. I. A. Publications, 1989).

objective of Gordon's sequence, the tools it involves have essentially no meaning unless students can attach them to some prior musical "sense" or understanding.

Gordon's music learning sequence has two components. The first, *discrimination learning,* is a rote–learning component that establishes the basis for audiation and subsequent music learning. During discrimination learning, students acquire the knowledge they will use later to make inferences about unfamiliar music. There are five levels of discrimination learning: (1) aural/oral learning, (2) verbal association learning, (3) partial synthesis learning, (4) symbolic association learning, and (5) composite synthesis learning. At the verbal association level, students learn to associate movable do syllables with melodic sounds and Gordon's rhythm syllables (see Figure 5–4) with rhythmic sounds and patterns.[12]

The second component of the music learning sequence is *inference learning,* in which students use discrimination learning as the basis for making sense of new or unfamiliar music. They basically teach themselves by making inferences about music that is new or unfamiliar after subconsciously comparing it with music they know. This second component of the music learning sequence has three levels: (1) generalization learning, (2) creativity or improvisation learning, and (3) theoretical understanding.[13]

PRINCIPLES OF LEARNING

A *principle* is a rule based on the best available evidence. As with all scientific truths, principles change as knowledge advances. But having surveyed a number of learning theories in some detail here and discussed how to organize, deliver, and evaluate instruction, this section concludes by stating learning principles[14] derived from all of these theories and methods of instruction. Music learning is facilitated under the following conditions:

1. Music activities are appropriate for students' physical, intellectual, and social maturity levels.
2. Teachers have faith in students' ability to learn and make it possible for them to achieve at optimal levels.
3. Teachers arrange for musical problems to be solved by the students.
4. Students have satisfying, enjoyable, and educational musical experiences.
5. There is a planned and sequential but flexible program of music instruction from one grade level to the next.
6. Students receive individualized, specific, frequent, sequential, varied, and appropriately spaced practice.
7. Teachers and parents work together to help students learn.
8. Students have good role models (other children, parents, teachers, other adults).

[12] Gordon, *Learning Sequences in Music: Skill, Content, and Patterns,* 20–49.

[13] Ibid., 49–61.

[14] Learning principles included here are derived from those found in Robert Evans Nye and Vernice Trousdale Nye, *Music in the Elementary School,* 5th ed. (Englewood Cliffs, NJ: Prentice Hall, 1985), 44–46.

Rhythm Syllables for Simple Meter

Rhythm Symbol	Edwin Gordon	Zoltán Kodály	Traditional Method
♩	Du	Ta	One
♫	Du da	Ti ti	One and
♬♬	Du ta de ta	Ti ri ti ri	One e–and–a
♩♬ (eighth, two sixteenths)	Du de ta	Ti ti ri	One and–a
♬♩ (two sixteenths, eighth)	Du da de	Ti ri ti	One–e and
(sixteenth eighth sixteenth)	Du ta ta	Ti ri ti	One–e a
(dotted eighth, sixteenth)	Du ta	Ti ri	One a
(sixteenth, dotted eighth)	Du ta	Ti ri	One–e
𝅗𝅥	Du	Ta a	One Two
(dotted quarter, eighth)	Du de	Ta i ti	One (Two) and
(eighth, dotted quarter)	Du de	Ti ta	One and (two and)
(eighth quarter eighth)	Du de de	Syn–co–pa	One and and
𝅗𝅥.	Du	Ta a a	One Two Three
𝅝	Du	Ta a a a	One Two Three Four

Rhythm Syllables for Compound Meter

Rhythm Symbol	Edwin Gordon	Zoltán Kodály	Traditional Method
♩.	Du	Ta	One
♪♪♪	Du da di	Ti ti ti	One and a OR one–la–lee
♬♬♬	Du ta da ta di ta	Ti ri ti ri ti ri	One ta la ta lee ta
(eighth two sixteenths eighth)	Du ta da di	Ti ri ti ti	One ta la lee
(eighth two sixteenths eighth)	Du da ta di	Ti ti ri ti	One la ta lee
(dotted eighth sixteenth eighth)	Du ta di	Ti ri ti	One ta lee

FIGURE 5–4   *Source:* Adapted from Grant Newman, *Teaching Children Music* (Dubuque, IA: Wm. C. Brown Publishers, 1989), 316.

9. Learning styles, levels of proficiency, and aptitudes are recognized and accommodated.

10. Students see meaning and relevance in what they are doing by making immediate practical use of skills and procedures, helping to establish long-range goals, suggesting activities and instructional materials, and participating in the evaluation process.

11. Teachers know in advance what they need to teach, how they are going to teach it, what they expect of students during and after instruction, and how they will measure the effectiveness of instruction.

12. Students are taught to ask different types of questions and are encouraged and given opportunities to use and develop this questioning skill.

13. Teachers plan musical activities that allow students to be successful.

14. Students are intrinsically motivated and personally involved in learning.

15. Students experience music through a combination of senses—touching, visually examining, hearing, and using the body and muscles for rhythmic interpretation.

16. Musical knowledge and skills are presented in logical sequence.

17. Learners are free to profit from making mistakes in a nonthreatening atmosphere.

18. There is consistent teacher-student evaluation and positive reinforcement from teacher and peers.

19. Students experience music actively, by singing, moving, listening, improvising, and playing musical instruments, before verbal descriptions and symbols are introduced.

20. Music learning is viewed as a cumulative process requiring repeated, meaningful experiences.

21. Expository and interactive teaching methods are used appropriately (depending upon what is being taught).

22. Students' command of music learning tools allows them to become independent learners.

23. Previously learned concepts are associated and combined with new ones: Students are allowed to discover what they already know and progress from there.

24. Students have the opportunity to work in more than one class format.

25. Students understand clearly what is to be learned, how it is to be learned, and how the learning will be evaluated.

STUDY AND DISCUSSION QUESTIONS

1. Read each of the following scenarios; then do the following: (a) Tell which one demonstrates "schooling" and which one demonstrates "education" as discussed in the introduction to Part II. Justify your answers. (b) Discuss the learner and "teacher" in each scenario in light of information included in this and the two preceding chapters.

ILLUSTRATION 1

When Russ gets his essay back from Mr. Kennedy, he notices that many misspelled words are circled. He sighs and slips the essay in his binder; he was never good at spelling anyway.

Midway through class, Mr. Kennedy comments that a number of students had problems with spelling on the essay assignment and that some of the same misspelled words appeared in several papers. He asks the class to repeat after him: *i* before *e* except after *c*. The class repeats the rule, then Mr. Kennedy asks the students to take out a scrap piece of paper and think about the rule as they write down the following words: *receive, believe, relieve, receipt, belief, mischief, conceive.*

Later that evening, Russ looks over his graded essay and notices that the new rule learned in class applies to some of the words he misspelled. He whispers the rule to himself and rewrites each word correctly.

ILLUSTRATION 2

At the beginning of the school day, when Jason opens his locker, his algebra book falls out, followed by his history book and finally his chemistry lab notebook. He greets his friend Sam, picks the books up off the floor, and places them back in the locker.

At lunch time, Jason opens his locker to get his lunch. Again his algebra book falls out, followed by his history book and his chemistry lab notebook. Jason continues talking to his friends Mary and Donald as he picks the books up off the floor and starts to place them back in the locker. Mary stops him and takes the books. She then places the thick algebra book directly on the shelf and puts the history book and then the thin chemistry notebook on top. The three students continue talking as Jason closes the locker.

At dismissal, Jason opens his locker; none of the books fall out. "Ummmm," he says as he closes the locker and starts for home.

2. Do aspects of one's teaching (e.g., instructional method, materials, evaluation) reflect a philosophical perspective? Explain your answer.

3. Based on what you know about the following listed education practices, discuss each one in light of information presented in this chapter. Consider such issues as accommodating learning styles, motivation, expository versus interactive teaching, and feedback mechanisms.

   music memory contests   singing schools
   rote-song method   self-instruction music manuals
   the Lancasterian system   required choral singing

4. You are meeting a seventh-grade general music class next week for the first time. One of the instructional objectives for this class session is to present the quarter rest. (The students learned quarter notes, eighth notes, and half notes last semester before their teacher retired.) Write a lesson plan for a ten-minute activity to help students achieve this objective. Use the lesson-plan strategy presented in this chapter as a guide. Your plan must include a complete behavioral objective.

5. Two students come to you for private instruction on your principal instrument. Both are beginners, are in the same fourth-grade class at school, and have had general music classes once a week since first grade. Sara has experimented with her brother's instrument and has taught herself to play a few simple melodies by ear. Sebastian has never played an instrument, but he's eager to learn. What would each student's first lesson with you be like? Consider the following:
   a. What do you already know about each student that should influence your instructional decisions?
   b. Should they learn the same things, in the same way, in the same sequence? Justify your response, using examples as appropriate.
   c. What goals might you establish for each student for the first four lessons?

REFERENCES AND RECOMMENDED SOURCES

CHOKSY, LOIS.   *The Kodály Context: Creating an Environment for Musical Learning.* Englewood Cliffs, NJ: Prentice Hall, 1981.

————.   *The Kodály Method: Comprehensive Music Education from Infant to Adult.* 2d ed. Englewood Cliffs, NJ: Prentice Hall, 1988.

————, and others.   *Teaching Music in the Twentieth Century.* Englewood Cliffs, NJ: Prentice Hall, 1986.

FINDLAY, ELSA.   *Rhythm and Movement: Applications of Dalcroze Eurhythmics.* Princeton, NJ: Summy–Birchard Music, 1971.

Gordon, Edwin.   "Gordon on Gordon." *The Quarterly* 2 (1991), 6–9.

————.   *Learning Sequences in Music: Skill, Content, and Patterns.* Chicago: G. I. A. Publications, 1980; reprint, Chicago: G. I. A. Publications, 1989.

HERMANN, EVELYN.   *Shinichi Suzuki: The Man and His Philosophy.* Athens, OH: Ability Development Associates, 1981.

KOPPELMAN, DORIS.   *Introducing Suzuki Piano.* San Diego, CA: Dichter Press, 1978.

LABUTA, JOSEPH A.   *Guide to Accountability in Music Instruction.* West Nyack, NJ: Parker Publishing Company, 1974; copyright assigned to Joseph A. Labuta, 1991.

LANDIS, BETH, AND POLLY CARTER.   *The Eclectic Curriculum in American Music Education: Contributions of Dalcroze, Kodaly, and Orff.* Washington, DC: Music Educators National Conference, 1972.

MARK, MICHAEL L.   *Contemporary Trends in Music Education.* 2d ed. New York: Schirmer Books, 1986.

NEWMAN, GRANT.   *Teaching Children Music.* Dubuque, IA: Wm. C. Brown Publishers, 1989.

NYE, ROBERT EVANS, AND VERNICE TROUSDALE NYE.   *Music in the Elementary School.* 5th ed. Englewood Cliffs, NJ: Prentice Hall, 1985.

SALIBA, KONNIE K.   *Accent on Orff: An Introductory Approach.* Englewood Cliffs, NJ: Prentice Hall, 1991.

SPECTOR, IRWIN.   *Rhythm and Life: The Work of Emile Jaques–Dalcroze.* Dance and Music Series. Stuyvesant, NY: Pendragon Press, 1990.

STANLEY SADIE, ED.   *The New Grove Dictionary of Music and Musicians.* London: Macmillan Publishers, 1980.

SUZUKI, SHINICHI.   *Nurtured by Love.* 2d ed. Trans. Waltraud Suzuki. Smithtown, NY: Exposition Press, 1983.

University of Northern Colorado.   *The Quarterly* 2 (1991), ed. Manny Brand.

WATERS, DARREL L., AND CYNTHIA CRUMP TAGGART.   *Readings in Music Learning Theory.* Chicago: G. I. A. Publications, 1989.

PART III

Music Education: Toward the Future

In 1983 the U.S. public first read a document that has since become one of the most discussed and quoted appraisals of U.S. education. This commentary on national and educational health was issued by the National Commission on Excellence in Education and set in motion a wave of educational change that is still rippling. Thus, this final section of the text is about transformation.

Chapter 6 examines current trends in American education and describes a variety of organizational and curricular changes that have occurred in recent years, most of which can be attributed to the commission's sixty-five-page document. As a general rule the current status of music education is not discussed separately because many events in its development are directly related to more general changes in education. Specific mention of music education is made when appropriate, but on the whole, changes relevant to this discipline are covered adequately by the general discussion.

Readers should also note that, although Chapter 6 presents numerous transformations in educational structure and content, the overriding purpose of schooling—to sustain societal well-being and perpetuate society's progress—remains a matter of consensus. Changes stemming from a resurgence of past ideas are explored alongside more radical ones generated by new convictions, but in no instance is the purpose of education questioned.

Changes discussed in Chapter 6 have generated considerable excitement for many education professionals and informed U.S. citizens, but they are a source of concern for others who wonder where they will lead. This is the topic of Chapter 7, in which all previously presented information is brought to bear on speculation about the future of U.S. education and about music education's role in schooling in the twenty-first century.

6

American Education Since 1980

INTRODUCTION AND OBJECTIVES

According to some, American society has been in decline since the 1960s. This decline is usually attributed to the counterculture that developed toward the end of that decade. As baby boomers who had come of age rejected insular containment policies, their quest for the good life, for meaning through intimacy, and for national and personal liberation took them beyond boundaries established by the previous generation. Political activism and rebellion replaced apathy and personal adaptation. Living together, divorce, and promiscuity replaced marriage and notions of the ideal American family. Risk taking replaced security seeking. Eccentricity and personal expression replaced conformity. Since the late sixties, escalating drug abuse and crime rates, corruption in government and private enterprise, movies and television shows bordering on pornography, teenage sexual activity, and profane and sexually explicit record lyrics along with questionable standards of advertising in mass media suggest that the nation is still in trouble.

In the process of ferreting out reasons for the persistence of the country's problems, national attention has turned once more to education. A call for reform has been under way since the 1970s, with scores of publications detailing the short-comings of public schools and offering suggestions for improvement. Amid this proliferation of critiques, one report surfaced to become the foundation of much that is currently being done in the way of educational reform.

The National Commission on Excellence in Education was organized in 1981 by Terrell Bell, then U.S. Secretary of Education, to study the quality of education in the United States and to report its findings to the public. The commission's report, *A Nation at Risk: The Imperative for Educational Reform,* published in 1983, began with the following statement:

Our nation is at risk. Our once unchallenged preeminence in commerce, industry, science, and technological innovation is being overtaken by competitors throughout the world. This report is concerned with only one of the many causes and dimensions of the problem, but it is the one that undergirds American prosperity, security, and civility. We report to the American people that while we can take justifiable pride in what our schools and colleges have historically accomplished and contributed to the United States and the well-being of its people, the educational foundations of our society are presently being eroded by a rising tide of mediocrity that threatens our very future as a Nation and a people. What was unimaginable a generation ago has begun to occur—others are matching and surpassing our educational attainments.[1]

In addition to being at risk of losing its competitive edge in international enterprises as a result of pervasive mediocrity, America was also at risk of losing the unity that its moral, spiritual, and intellectual strengths had forged since its founding. These were prophetic words.

This chapter explores developments in U.S. education since 1980. Changes are occurring so rapidly that much of this information may be dated by the time it is read, but these events convey important lessons; it is easier to understand why things are as they are when one understands how they evolved.

Chapter 6 will enable readers to do the following:

- Discuss developments in general education and in music education since the 1980s.
- Name at least three societal or cultural developments that have occurred since 1980 and describe each one's effect on general or music education.
- List and describe at least four current trends in education and explain their effects on music education.

EDUCATION REFORM SINCE 1980

Two kinds of reform plans have been apparent in the U.S. since 1980.[2] Conservative and traditional reform plans seek to make changes incrementally and within the current educational structure. They emphasize notions inherent in public schooling. Government retains control of the education process on two levels: As *provider* of the service, it sets policies and objectives for education; as *producer* of the service, it determines the manner in which these policies and objectives are enforced and attained. In addition, and no doubt because of the nature of public enterprise in a democratic society, homogeneity and commonality are two of these plans' salient features. Education generally proceeds in the same way in all schools, under the same kinds of supervision, within the same types of facilities, and employing the same methods. Diversity is discouraged rather than encouraged.

---

[1] National Commission on Excellence in Education, *A Nation at Risk: The Imperative for Educational Reform*, a report to the Nation and the U.S. Secretary of Education (Washington, DC: Government Printing Office, 1983), 5.

[2] See Chester E. Finn and Herbert J. Walberg, eds., *Radical Education Reforms* (Berkeley, CA: McCutchan Publishing Corporation, 1994); and Myron Lieberman, *Privatization and Educational Choice* (New York: St. Martin's Press, 1989).

Educational services are provided by public officials and employees in public facilities. Because educational profits or expenditures are the public's gain or its burden, there is also an overriding concern with means: how the system is structured, how much the public is investing in it, how services are delivered. Moreover, education under more traditional plans tends to be insular. Corporate, community, and other interests are usually kept at arm's length from school operations. The government, as producer and provider of education, dominates; dissatisfied taxpayers have limited options and circumscribed recourse.

Since the late 1970s, however, the idea of public schooling has been challenged not only by religious groups seeking public support for their educational institutions but by reformers who envision schools that could be public and yet varied. Such nontraditional reform plans support heterogeneity and experimentation. Districts, communities, and schools, along with teachers, parents, and students, are encouraged to devise educational schemes that will achieve desired outcomes using whatever means required by their young people's particular circumstances and needs.

Radical and nontraditional reforms seek to make sweeping or drastic educational changes and move in new directions.[3] These plans encourage collaboration among teachers, parents, educational institutions, and businesses within a given community. Whereas traditional plans stress means, nontraditional ones focus on ends: Education is viewed as an outcome rather than a process or system and is only considered effective if the desired outcomes result. Education consumers (students, parents, the general public) are given considerably more choice about who will deliver education services, and their choices are based on provider effectiveness, as determined by educational outcomes. In this way, providers are held accountable for what they do or do not achieve. The education "market" becomes competitive: those who can compete prosper, whereas those who can't compete (as a result of the quality or price of their product) don't survive. Thus, key concepts underlying most radical educational proposals are *privatization* and *educational choice*.

Choice in Education

Educational choice allows parents to decide which schools their children will attend rather than having this be determined by school district boundaries or by where they live. Thus educational choice involves complex and controversial issues related to public versus private schooling, educational funding, and deregulation. Choice plans enacted in different parts of the country attempt to accommodate varying, often conflicting perspectives on these issues by using one or more practical ideas related to privatization.

Privatization (the transfer of all or partial responsibility for producing a service from the public to the private sector) is currently an international trend, but it is not a new idea. Rather, different countries have used privatization for centuries, albeit under different

---

[3] Joseph L. Bast and Herbert J. Walberg, "Free Market Choice: Can Education Be Privatized?" in Chester E. Finn and Herbert J. Walberg, eds., *Radical Education Reforms* (Berkeley, CA: McCutchan Publishing Corporation, 1994), 153. Drucker calls these governmental functions "governing" and "doing," respectively. See Peter Drucker, *The Age of Discontinuity: Guidelines to Our Changing Society* (New York: Harper and Row, 1968; reprint, New Brunswick, NJ: Transaction Publishers, 1992), 233–242.

names and often for a variety of services. In the U.S., the current trend toward privatization in education amounts to reversing past reassignments of responsibility, just as transportation and sewage are "public" services that began as private, for-profit ventures. Prior to the 1830s, education usually involved dealings between consumers and nonpublic contractors. Today, state and federal governments replace private citizens and groups in educational enterprises so that the government is the foremost producer and provider of American education. Most industrialized nations encourage and support educational privatization, and a similar trend is apparent in Russian education.

The general theory underlying educational privatization states that making education an enterprise in which providers compete for consumers will necessarily improve the quality and cost-efficiency of the commodity, as evidenced by outcomes rather than systems. In most instances, it is too early to determine whether this is true, but there is every reason to believe that a system in which citizens take an active role will be more effective than one over which they have limited control. Because enrollment determines school funding, any school that lost students as a result of its poor quality would experience drastically reduced resources, even in districts in which privatization and choice plans operate alongside public schooling. Competitive schools would experience increased enrollments, increased funding, and would thus remain economically solvent.

In business, privatization involves *load shedding* (turning over partial responsibility for a service to private interests or contractors), *contracting out* (accepting bids for providing a service and awarding the contract to the "best" bidder), and *accountability* (producers being responsible for achieving, or failing to achieve, outcomes specified in their agreements with consumers).[4] Most proposed educational reforms—voucher systems, empowerment and site-based management, alternative or magnet programs, home schooling, and charter schools—use practical ideas derived from each of these.

Voucher Systems and Charter Schools

Vouchers stand for government money that public schools receive for each student enrolled in them. Because the majority of children attending public schools have to enroll in the school nearest their home, this money usually goes to these children's neighborhood school—regardless of the quality of educational experiences it offers. Private and parochial schools do not receive government money for students they enroll. Under proposed voucher systems, however, parents would be able to enroll their children in any public or private school in their district regardless of its location if they believed that school offered the best educational opportunities. Most of these proposals also recommend that private and parochial schools receive government money for students enrolled in them.

Voucher choice plans are highly controversial. Whereas proponents suggest that these systems will generate competition and accountability that will improve education, detractors of voucher plans maintain that government funding of sectarian education and the potential erosion of public schooling are reasons for concern. Even so, a number of

---

[4] See Myron Lieberman, *Privatization and Educational Choice* (New York: St. Martin's Press, 1989).

school districts throughout the country have implemented voucher systems on a limited basis, and many of these plans have met with some success. For example, the Milwaukee Parental Choice Program (MPCP), which began in 1990, is funded by the state of Wisconsin. Under this system, the state of Wisconsin allocates approximately $2,500 annually to a limited number of qualified students attending private schools that qualify for the voucher program under carefully proscribed and detailed criteria.

Charter schools are independent public schools designed and operated by concerned parents, teachers, school administrators, private corporations, or individuals. Although they "operate under charters or contracts with school districts, state education agencies, or other public institutions,"[5] charter schools receive considerable autonomy from district, state, and union requirements regarding curriculum, instruction, budget, and personnel matters. Most of them also receive the average government expenditure for each student enrolled, with some receiving $5,000 or more per pupil. In return for this freedom and funding, they agree to be accountable for student achievement, abide by antidiscrimination mandates, and provide nonsectarian instruction.[6]

In 1991, Minnesota became the first state to enact charter school legislation, but between 1991 and 1995, ten other states (Arizona, California, Colorado, Georgia, Hawaii, Kansas, Massachusetts, Michigan, New Mexico, and Wisconsin) instituted charter school laws. Nine of these eleven states had approved 131 charter school proposals as of January 1995, and 88 of these approved charter schools were in operation.

Charter schools offer students and parents a wide range of educational choices because although the structure and educational offerings of many charter schools are quite similar to those of traditional schools, many other charter schools implement innovative curricula and ideas suggested by some of this nation's prominent education critics. For instance, the Academy Charter School (kindergarten through eighth grade) is one of two schools in Colorado that follow former U.S. Secretary of Education William Bennett's James Madison elementary school model. Jingletown Charter Middle School in Oakland, California, accommodates students who speak English as a second language. Teachers in this school adapt their use of English to their students' level of English proficiency but follow California's core curriculum, focusing on content rather than language acquisition. Central Park East Secondary School (grades 7 through 12) in New York City is one of several high-school affiliates of Theodore Sizer's Coalition of Essential Schools,[7] and two

---

[5] Health, Education, and Human Services Division, *Charter Schools: New Model for Public Schools Provides Opportunities and Challenges.* Report to Congressional Registers (Gaitherburg, MD: U.S. General Accounting Office, 1995), 3, ERIC, ED 378 702.

[6] See Donna Harrington-Leuker, "Charter Schools," *American School Board Journal* 181 (September 1994), 22–26; and Donna Harrington-Leuker, "Charter 'Profit'," *American School Board Journal* (September 1994), 27–28. Charter school laws vary from state to state, but these provisions and requirements are included in most of them.

[7] The Coalition of Essential Schools (CES) was developed by Theodore R. Sizer at Brown University in 1984 as a school-university partnership to promote high school reform. As of 1994, 550 schools throughout the U.S. were affiliated with CES. See Tony Wagner, *How Schools Change: Lessons from Three Communities* (Boston, MA: Beacon Press, 1994); Theodore R. Sizer, *Horace's School: Redesigning the American High School* (Boston, MA: Houghton Mifflin, 1992); and George Wood, *Schools that Work: America's Most Innovative Public Education Programs* (New York: NAL, 1992).

grade schools in Colorado use the curriculum proposed by Mortimer J. Adler and the Paideia Group.[8]

Like voucher systems, reform plans including charter schools are controversial. Teachers in some school districts believe that charter schools will eventually break their unions. Concerned citizens in education and the general population worry that, considering limits most states have set on the number of charter schools that may operate at any given time, there will not be enough charter schools to have a significant effect upon the quality of U.S. public education. There is also general concern that these schools may become forums for special interest groups. The National Association of School Boards' (NASB) conservative support of charter schools reflects all of these concerns: NASB only endorses charter schools in states in which local school boards control granting and revoking charters.

Some charter schools' independence from school districts also raises questions about how states should treat these schools regarding federal programs and requirements such as those for Title I and special education. An important issue is whether legally independent charter schools are local education agencies (LEAS) as defined by the federal government.[9] If independent charter schools attain LEA status, they would operate their own Title I programs and be eligible for state Title I funds. In spite of this caution and uncertainty, however, the charter school movement continues to gather momentum.

Contracting Out

When *contracting out* a service (paying a person, group, or agency for its services), a consumer accepts bids for the service from several providers and awards the service contract to the provider whose offer is most satisfactory. (Some managed health care in the U.S. operates on a contractual basis.) In education, contracting out will allow a variety of public and private organizations to operate schools on the basis of school-specific contracts defining each school's mission, guaranteeing a certain amount of public finding, and specifying the terms of accountability.[10] The most controversial contracting proposal of the current educational reform movement is the Edison Project[11] developed by Chris Whittle, chairman of Whittle Communications Inc., Knoxville, Tennessee.

---

[8] Ibid., 26; Deborah Meier, "Central Park East: An Alternative Story," *Skole* 4–8 (1988—1992), 122–134, ed. Mary M. Leue, ERIC, ED 360 126; Theodore R. Sizer, "Rebuilding: First Steps," *Skole* 4–8 (1988–1992), 135–148, ed. Mary M. Leue, ERIC, ED 360 126; Mortimer J. Adler, *The Paideia Proposal: An Educational Manifesto* (New York: Macmillan Publishing, 1982); Mortimer J. Adler, *The Paideia Proposal: An Educational Syllabus* (New York: Macmillan Publishing, 1984); Mortimer J. Adler, *Paideia Problems and Possibilities* (New York: Macmillan Publishing Co., 1983); and William J. Bennett, *Our Country and Our Children* (New York: Simon and Schuster, 1988).

[9] Health, Education, and Human Services Division, *Charter Schools: New Model for Public Schools Provides Opportunities and Challenges,* 5–6. Also see Donna Harrington-Lueker, "Charter 'Profit'," *American School Board Journal* (September 1994), 27–28 for indepth discussion of controversy surrounding Michigan's first charter school, which is designed to operate as a distance learning network for home schoolers.

[10] Paul T. Hill, "Reinventing Urban Public Education," *Phi Delta Kappan* 75 (January 1994), 397.

[11] The Edison Project gets its name from Thomas Alva Edison (1847–1931) whose late-nineteenth-century inventions included the electric lamp, the motion picture projector, and the phonograph. See Marilee C. Rist, "Here Comes 'McSchool'," *American School Board Journal* 178 (September 1991), 30–31.

According to Deborah McGriff, senior vice president of Edison, the project consists of 100 people from education, business, science, and other fields who have formulated a comprehensive, integrated, and research-based curriculum design.[12] The Edison design accommodates children from ages 3 through 18 and deviates from traditional education in a number of ways: (1) Students attend school 210 days per year rather than 180, and schools are open from 7:00 a.m. until 6:00 p.m. each weekday for optional enrichment activities; (2) all children in primary grades learn Spanish and those in higher grades study Latin; and (3) students receive interdisciplinary instruction built around health and physical fitness, humanities and the arts, science and mathematics, character and ethics, and practical arts and skills.[13]

School districts entering into a partnership with the Edison Project agree to pay approximately $5,500 per student, the national average per-pupil cost for public education. (Edison determines the exact per-pupil expenditure for each school district by analyzing factors such as the district's overall budget, school enrollments, and teacher salaries.) In return for this payment, districts can expect the project to do the following for each of its schools that the contract covers: (1) Manage and administer educational programs and personnel matters; (2) maintain and operate school buildings; (3) make any building adaptations necessary for implementing the program, including installing extensive technological equipment; (4) provide start-up money for such things as curriculum development, technology systems, and staff recruitment and development; and (5) be responsible for transportation and food service. Most important, contracts with the Edison Project include clear performance standards, and the project will be accountable for meeting them.[14]

Chris Whittle revised his initial goal—to open 200 schools in the fall of 1996—because of financial difficulties met with in 1994 by Whittle Communications, Inc. (The Edison Project is independent of Whittle Communications, Inc., but its operation relies heavily upon Whittle's financial support.) In addition, the project's research, development, and marketing phase cost $40 million—two-thirds of the total amount initially alloted for this phase and the project's implementation phase combined. Whittle and the Edison Project had to raise between $25 and $50 million in order to implement their design. In December 1995, the Edison Project confirmed its plan to open an elementary school in Mt. Clemens, Michigan, in the fall of 1996. Negotiations with the Renaissance Elementary (Charter) School in Boston, Massachusetts, were nearly complete, and contracts with several school districts (Wichita, Kansas; Sherman, Texas, Dade County, Florida; Colorado Springs, Colorado) were pending.[15]

Most controversy surrounding the Edison Project focuses on Whittle's education-for-profit perspective, his financial solvency, the project's apparent lack of provisions for children with special needs, and the project's preferred per-pupil fee, which may prohibit many interested school districts from forming partnerships with it. Some people believe, however, that regardless of the outcome of the Edison Project, "the level of discourse

---

[12] Judith Brody Saks, "Scrutinizing Edison," *American School Board Journal* 182 (February 1995), 22.

[13] Ibid., 22–23.

[14] Ibid., 21–22.

[15] Ibid., 21.

about education [in the United States] has been raised"[16] and this will ultimately improve the education available to all children.

Magnet Programs

Alternative education is not a new idea in the United States.[17] Parochial schools instituted during the nineteenth century offered Catholic Americans an alternative to common or public schools just as John Dewey's progressive Laboratory School (established in 1896 in Chicago) and *open schools* (schools without walls based on A. S. Neill's educational philosophy and organized during the 1960s and 1970s)[18] also offered educational alternatives to parents and students. During the early 1970s, however, when it became clear that alternative programs could "act as [magnets] to attract children from throughout the school district,"[19] these programs became means of desegregating schools naturally and avoiding forced integration by way of court-ordered bussing as mandated by the Supreme Court's decision in *Swann v. Charlotte-Mecklenbury Board of Education* (1971). Thus, alternative programs gradually became known as *magnet programs.*

Although current magnet programs are usually integration strategies, they are also a means of achieving consumer choice in arts education. Fine arts magnet programs emphasize the visual and literary arts, music, drama, and dance and offer students a depth and breadth of arts instruction not usually available in traditional school programs. The format, admission policies, and objectives of these programs vary, however. Students enrolled in schools with fine arts *enrichment programs* complete the school's basic curriculum but may elect one or two special arts enrichment courses each term. In some instances, these enrichment classes are offered before or after school rather than during the school day. *Magnet programs in schools* (sometimes referred to as schools within schools) are similar to enrichment programs, but students participating in these spend more regular school hours in arts classes.

Magnet schools, a third format used for fine arts alternative programs, are structured in one of two ways. In some of these schools, the arts serve as a theme for entire curriculum: All teachers in the school infuse the arts in the subjects they teach.[20] In other fine arts magnet schools, particularly those focusing on preprofessional training, students spend

[16] Ibid., 25.

[17] See Joel Spring, *The American School: 1642–1990,* 342, 352, 366–68; Marilyn von Seggern, "Magnet Music Programs: A Look at the Issues, "*Music Educators Journal* (March 1990), 50–53; Jo Anna Natale, "The Attraction of the Arts," *Music Educators Journal* (December 1992), 46–48.

[18] See A. S. Neill, *Summerhill: A Radical Approach to Child Rearing,* with a foreword by Erich Fromm (New York: Pocket Books, 1960); and Ewald B. Nyquist and Gene R. Hawes, eds., *Open Education: A Sourcebook for Parents and Teachers* (New York: Bantam Books, 1972).

[19] Spring, *The American School: 1642–1990,* 368.

[20] Sharon L. Newhill, *The Paseo Fine and Performing Arts Magnet High School, 1989–1990, 1990–1991, 1991–1992: Summative Evaluation* (Kansas City, MO: Kansas City School District, 1992), 14, ERIC, ED 380 387.

one-half of each day or more in arts courses. Fiorello H. LaGuardia High School of Performing Arts in New York City (the oldest fine arts magnet school in the U.S.) and the Booker T. Washington High School for the Performing and Visual Arts in Dallas exemplify this intensive type of program.

There are also a dozen or so residential magnet high schools in the U.S. that attract students from across the country. Two such schools—the Virginia School of the Arts in Lynchburg and the Harid Conservatory in Boca Raton, Florida—offer intensive preprofessional training and numerous performance opportunities, many of which are in collaboration with professional artists.[21]

Admission procedures for magnet programs vary according to each program's format and objectives. Whereas enrichment programs typically admit students on a first-come-first-served or lottery basis, the more intensive and specialized magnet schools require that students successfully complete an audition. Many fine arts programs do not require previous training, however, so their auditions assess potential, attitude, and level of commitment to the arts rather than achievement.

Requirements for continued participation in these programs also vary. Frequently, the first year of enrollment in the program is probationary, and students may only enroll for a second year if they make satisfactory academic and artistic progress while on probation. Some magnet programs also require that students maintain a specific grade point average. At Booker T. Washington High School, for instance, students must carry at least a C average in academic classes and a B average in their arts classes to stay in the program.[22]

Magnet school supporters point out that these schools frequently have positive effects on student achievement besides promoting school integration, educational innovation, and consumer choice.[23] Other people who are less certain about the effectiveness of magnet programs note that, in addition to being expensive to implement and maintain, these programs sometimes have negative effects on arts programs in more traditional schools. They also suggest that magnet programs can easily become performance-oriented and elitist programs.

Nevertheless, there were more than 200 public schools for the arts operating in school districts across the United States in 1992[24] and plans for others were underway. Largely because of the magnet school concept's popularity with parents and students, it appears that for now, this educational reform strategy is meeting some of society's needs.

[21] Muriel Topaz, "Something New Is in the Air: Arts Magnet High Schools," *Dance Magazine* (April 1995), 100–103. LaGuardia High School, the model for many American arts magnet programs, was also the basis for the 1980 movie "Fame."

[22] Ibid., 101.

[23] See Sharon L. Newhill, *The Paseo Fine and Performing Arts Magnet High School, 1989–1990, 1990–1991, 1991–1992: Summative Evaluation.*

[24] Jo Anna Natale, "The Attraction of the Arts," 46.

Home Schooling

Teaching children in the home is the oldest form of education. In its most informal and simplest form, *home schooling*[25] dates from the beginning of civilization. In formal instruction, it dates from classical Greece and Rome and was used extensively in America through the early common school period. During each of these periods, home schools were viable and accepted alternatives to the institutionalized schooling. In fact, many of this country's leaders were schooled at home to some degree. Home schooling never disappeared entirely, although there were periods when the number of children it affected fell markedly. Declines were usually short-lived, however, and in recent years, with the academic and moral quality of institutionalized schooling under attack, it has become an increasingly popular option.

Some people credit John Holt, American educator and home-school advocate, with sparking renewed interest in home schooling but most consider Raymond and Dorothy Moore of California the principal leaders of the modern home school movement.[26] Both are educators with extensive experience working with children at a variety of educational levels. Raymond Moore taught in public school and at the college level and served as a college vice-president and president before 1964, when he became graduate research and programs officer in the U.S. Office of Education. (He resigned the post three years later, disillusioned by the political nature of educational policy decisions.)

Moore and his wife became directly involved with home schooling in 1945 when their long-standing concern about formal education during the early childhood years prompted them to educate their children at home. Later, after establishing the research division of the Hewitt Foundation (known later as the Moore Foundation), they conducted research to determine the best age for children to begin formal schooling. Their theory, which they publicized through lectures, television, printed materials, and radio, was that young children were not cognitively or emotionally ready for formal instruction in school settings and that this premature experience during fragile and formative years could do irreparable harm. Home schooling became their preferred educational approach.

After the Moores began their work, home schooling gained considerable support, particularly during the 1980s. Accurate statistics are difficult to obtain (given the legal climate surrounding home schools), but estimates are that between 248,500 and 353,500 children were being educated at home during the 1990–1991 school year.[27] Many people expect this number to increase steadily to 500,000 or more by 1997 as growing numbers of

---

[25] The fact that this educational approach is called home "schooling" rather than home "education" underscores differences between inside- and outside-of-school teaching and learning, as discussed in the introduction to Part II of this text.

[26] See John W. Whitehead and Alexis Irene Crow, *Home Education: Rights and Reasons* (Wheaton IL: Crossway Books, 1993), 116–119; Patricia M. Lines, "Home Schooling," *ERIC Digest* (April 1995), ERIC, ED 381 849; and Patrick K. Aiex, *Home Schooling, Socialization, and Creativity in Children* (April 1994), ED 367 040.

[27] Patricia M. Lines, *Estimating the Home Schooled Population,* Working paper prepared for the Office of Education Research and Improvement (Washington, DC: U.S. Department of Education, 1991), ED 337 903.

parents become dissatisfied with public, private, or parochial schools and choose to educate their children themselves.[28]

Disenchantment with public schooling stems from any of several sources. The secular nature of institutionalized education; low academic standards; unsatisfactory curricular offerings; the social, moral, and cultural climate in schools; and the restrictive nature of commonly used teaching and classroom management methods are frequently cited rationales for starting in-home schools. Ultimately, however, parents may choose to instruct their children at home to have more control over the children's general upbringing. Decisions to home school may be a political response of people who are trying to defend a way of life that they believe is threatened by the existing organization and content of public education.[29]

Available data suggest that the average American home schooling family includes a father, a mother, and three children. Both parents have approximately two years of education beyond high school, and each of them takes an active role in educating the children although they are not certified teachers. The mother assumes most of the instructional responsibility, however, because the father is the family's primary provider, earning between $25,000 and $49,000 annually. The family attends a Christian or Protestant church on a regular basis.[30]

Generally, children who are educated at home spend 3–4 hours per day studying a wide range of traditional subjects such as mathematics, science, English or language arts, and history or social studies. The children's learning programs are flexible and individualized to accommodate their interests and temperaments, but many of them use a combination of homemade and purchased, sequential instructional materials. Physical education, music, art, geography, and health are important, but home schoolers define and prioritize these subjects differently. "It is up to them to decide what form 'physical education' will take, for example, and whether it is better to learn to play the piano or to learn art history."[31]

If children schooled at home are between the ages of 7 and 18, state mandates may require that they be tested annually using a nationally recognized standardized test such as the Metropolitan Achievement Test (MAT), the Cognitive Abilities Test (CAT), the Sequential Tests of Academic Progress, or the Scholastic Aptitude Test (SAT). When tested, children from home schools tend to score significantly higher than their peers in public schools (i.e., 3%–12% above the national average on the SAT and in the 70th and 80th percentiles on the CAT—approximately two percentiles higher than the national average for

---

[28] Ibid.; and *A National Study of Home Education* (Paeonian Springs, VA: Home School Legal Defense Association, 1990), 6, ERIC, ED 381 725.

[29] Maralee Mayberry, *Conflict and Social Determinisim: The Reprivitization of Education,* Paper presented at the annual meeting of the American Educational Research Association, Chicago, IL, 3–7 April 1991, 10, ERIC, ED 330 107.

[30] See *A National Study of Home Education;* and Brian D. Ray, "A Comparison of Home Schooling and Conventional Schooling with a Focus on Learner Outcomes," *Skole* 4–8 (1988—1992), 57, ed. Mary M. Leue, ERIC, ED 360 126.

[31] David Colfax and Micki Colfax, *Homeschooling for Excellence* (New York: Warner Books, 1988), 93.

this examination). In addition, these children have healthy self-concepts and demonstrate average to above-average social and psychological development.[32]

The definition of schools that is included in many states compulsory school attendance laws has been expanded to include home schooling, yet home schooling families are often involved in litigation with state education agencies. Pros and cons of educating children in the home continue to be debated, usually in the courtroom.

PEDAGOGICAL AND CURRICULAR TRENDS

In addition to recent changes in educational structure or format, schooling is being altered in significant ways by several other trends. The most prominent and far-reaching of these are discussed in this section.

Technology in Education

With the exception of television, recent technological advancements have contributed more to broadening access to information and knowledge and to increasing the number of education delivery systems than any development in recent times. Telecommunications and computers have combined to create the information superhighway, with its international network of libraries, data storage centers, financial institutions, and stock markets making access to information practically limitless. In addition, laser and compact disks, which accommodate incredible amounts of information in a virtually indestructible form, have altered information storage so that books and other traditional media may eventually be rarities.

Computer technology has been especially influential in education. As predicted by Moore's law (which estimated the rate at which computer chips would become more powerful), greatly expanded computer capabilities are no longer limited to the large, bulky mainframes of early computerization, nor are they restricted to computers systems in educational institutions or in workplaces. Microcomputer technology has developed to the point that personal computers, smaller notebook computers, and hand-held computer models are nearly as capable of sophisticated functions as their larger counterparts, and all of these have become increasingly affordable. One speculates that it is just a matter of time before even more compact models replace current mid-size and portable ones.

Given the impact of computers on society in general, it is not surprising that they have had so much influence on education. Whereas computer instruction a decade or so ago focused on developing computer literacy (teaching students about computers), current computer usage has turned toward actual instruction—either through *integrated learning systems* (ILS) that provide structured support for basic skills development or the less struc-

---

[32] Ibid. Also see Nola Kortner Aiex, "Home Schooling and Socialization of Children," *ERIC Digest* (1994), ED 372 460; Patricia M. Lines, "Home Schooling," *ERIC Digest* (April 1995), ED 381 849; and Robert Calvery, David Bell, and Carl Vaupel, *The Difference in Achievement between Home Schooled and Public Schooled Students in Grades Four, Seven, and Ten in Arkansas,* Paper presented at the annual meeting of the Mid-South Educational Research Association, Knoxville, TN (11–13 November 1992), ED 354 248.

tured *tool use approach,* which focuses on discovery learning, skill application, and more extensive interaction between the learner and the computer program.

Computer-assisted instruction (CAI) dates from the mid-1900s and was made available to schools a few years ago as a relatively new option. Today, it is used in many schools as a matter of course, and the use of CIA is expected to grow as computer programs become more interactive, flexible, and multimedia oriented. The Waterford Institute, a nonprofit organization established in New York City in 1976, has conducted considerable research relevant to using computers to support reading and math instruction in elementary schools. The institute now has offices in Utah, where it owns and operates a research school devoted to testing new concepts in computer instruction. It also has developed the Waterford Model, a school improvement program being used in elementary schools in New York City and offering a structured approach for using computer-assisted instruction (CAI).

Technology in Music Education

Technology's potential impact upon music education is greater as a result of recent developments having to do with sound reproduction, recording, and storage. Laser disks and compact disks generated far-reaching changes in the recording industry and have demonstrated their usefulness in music classrooms as the computer industry has shifted from focusing on computer-assisted instruction to enhancing the multimedia capabilities of technology.[33]

Computer use in music education has progressed from first-generation software using large mainframe computers to late fourth-generation software that uses 32-bit power to create a wealth of possibilities for music teachers and their students.[34] In addition, the Multiple Interface Digital Information (MIDI) protocol allows instruments, computers, and other media such as CD players, tape recorders to be connected to computers for use in a multitude of ways. Thus, in addition to CAI drill-and-practice programs that provide support for developing basic music reading and performance skills, more recent software enables students to create, orchestrate, notate, listen to, and edit compositions using the computer.

The increased flexibility of computer applications make computer technology a viable option for group as well as individual instruction.[35] Computer applications such as Vivace, Claire, Practica Musica, and MacGamut (all of which are for the Macintosh computer) are designed for group instruction but include menus and dialog boxes that allow teachers to "create a tailor-made curriculum for an individual or [a specific]

---

[33] See Brian Moore, "Future Technology: Working for Education," *Music Educators Journal* (November 1992), 30–32, 67.

[34] See G. David Peters, Music Software and Emerging Technology," *Music Educators Journal* (November 1992), 22-25, 63.

[35] See David Brian Williams, and Peter Richard Webster, *Experiencing Music Technology: Software, Data, and Hardware* (New York: Schirmer Books, 1996) for an in-depth discussion of computer technology and current music applications. Much of the information here is taken from this reference.

class"[36] and enable students to select and practice only those skills in which they are deficient.

Three other recently developed types of CIA software have helped to increase options available to music educators and their students. Computer programs such as Music/Ace and Pianist (both developed for Macintosh and Windows) and Explorations and Eine Kleine Nachtmusik (both designed for Macintosh) are *simulation* applications designed so that students' interaction with them through musical behaviors such as listening, creating, and performing are similar to actual music-making experiences. *Multimedia* programs bring text, graphics, audio and visual disk recordings, and animation together "to offer an unusually powerful and flexible environment for teaching about music."[37] These programs allow students to read data associatively and nonlinearly—in virtually any order—instead of having to read them in a preset, linear sequence. The third types of CAI computer programs are contentless applications called *instructional shells*. "That is to say, someone has already programmed the logic of the computer software but has left it empty of content so [users] can fill in [their] own information."[38] These shells enable teachers to develop learning packages that are appropriate for individuals and classes, and many of these applications accommodate multimedia programs. After the teacher or student fills them with data, these programs can be used for group and individual presentations.

The Yamaha Corporation of America's "Music In Education" provides an example of how multimedia applications can be used with groups. "Music in Education" is a technology-assisted multimedia program that combines keyboards, compact disks, an overhead projector, and a computer for group general music instruction. Its interactive software programs offer listening lessons for students to use individually or in small groups. These programs use the computer's improved color capabilities in conjunction with its improved graphics, sound reproduction features, and interactive abilities to present challenging activities through which students refine their listening skills while exploring and comparing compositions in the standard orchestral repertoire. By connecting computers to various playback and storage devices, teachers can quickly and easily develop multimedia examples for classroom use.

A Theory of Multiple Intelligences

Perhaps the most influential development in pedagogy, teaching, and learning since 1980 (other than advances in computer technology) has been the growing popularity of a revised theory of human aptitudes and abilities. This notion of multifaceted mind is not new. Rather, Howard Gardner has stimulated a resurgence of multidimensional thinking about

[36] Ibid., 87.
[37] Ibid., 88–89.
[38] Ibid., 19–20.

development and cognition.[39] He maintains that this pluralistic approach is a more accurate description of human functioning than the traditional unilineal scheme of abilities or skill domains.

According to Gardner and his colleagues, multiple intelligence theory blends the theoretical with the practical, the ethnocentric with the universal, the domain-specific (cognitive, affective, psychomotor) with the cross-modal, the genetic with the developmental. As such, it represents the most recent shift in philosophical and psychological thinking, a shift similar to that noted earlier with regard to theories of art before and after Baumgarten. Theories have evolved from viewing thought as an externally triggered process to seeing it as an internally generated one. Classical theorists focused on concrete external objects as represented in the mind. Enlightenment theorists focused on the mental or internal representations of these objects. Gardner and others focus on these internal representations and other mental "symbol" systems as initiators rather than merely products of thought.

As Gardner puts it, theorists who adopt this perspective seek to expand Piaget's ideas and methods to encompass symbol systems other than those normally considered when defining and measuring intelligence. Thus, *multiple intelligence*[40] theory sets forth seven intelligences or symbol systems, all of which are simultaneously ways of perceiving, interacting, processing, generating, behaving, responding, and manipulating. These intelligences are presented here in random order: (1) *linguistic,* characterized by sensitivity to sound, structure, meaning, and function in language; (2) *intrapersonal,* which focuses upon self-knowledge or understanding; (3) *logical-mathematical,* represented by an affinity for numerical and logical sequences; (4) *interpersonal,* marked by sensitivity to or understanding of others' feelings, moods, and so forth; (5) *spatial,* notably characterized by sensitivity to aspects of the visual-spatial world; (6) *musical,* characterized by sensitivity to sound, structure, and function of musical elements; and (7) *bodily-kinesthetic,* characterized by physical self-knowledge and understanding of the body's parts as related to each other and of the body as it relates to other objects.

According to the multiple intelligence theory, all human beings have some degree of aptitude for each intelligence and an elevated aptitude in at least one of them. One of Gardner's objectives has been to examine implications of this theory for education. In his opinion

> it should be possible to identify an individual's intellectual profile (or proclivities) at an early age and then draw upon this knowledge to enhance that person's educational opportunities and options. One could channel individuals with unusual talents into special programs, even

---

[39] See Howard Gardner, *Frames of Mind: The Theory of Multiple Intelligences* (New York: Basic Books, 1983), paperback ed. with Introduction by Howard Gardner (New York: Basic Books, 1985); Howard Gardner, *Multiple Intelligences: The Theory in Practice* (New York: Basic Books, 1993); and Thomas Armstrong, *Multiple Intelligences in the Classroom* (Alexandria, VA: Association for Supervision and Curriculum Development, 1994).

[40] Gardner generally defines *intelligence* as "the ability to solve problems, or to create products, that are valued within one or more cultural settings."

as one could devise prosthetics and special enrichment programs for individuals presenting an atypical or a dysfunctional profile of intellectual competences.[41]

As this theory has gained acceptance, it has changed the way many educators and institutions approach instruction. The profession must move cautiously, but the potential contributions of multiple intelligence theory to formal education are exciting and certainly merit thorough investigation.

Teacher Preparation and Certification

Teaching was cited in *A Nation At Risk* as one of four "disturbing inadequacies" of schooling that were contributing to the declining educational performance of American youth.[42] Regarding teacher preparation, the National Commission on Excellence in Education concluded that: (1) the teaching profession was not attracting enough "academically able students"—too often, preservice teachers came from the lowest quarter of their high school and college class; and (2) college preparation for teachers devoted too much time to how to teach and not enough time to strengthening knowledge of subject matter or content. The commission then recommended that the following be done to improve teacher preparation: (1) preservice teachers should be held to high educational standards and demonstrate competence in their academic discipline, and college programs should be evaluated on the basis of their graduating students having met these requirements; and (2) education officials and teachers should formulate "career ladders" to distinguish among "the beginning teacher, the experienced teacher, and the master teacher."[43]

Subsequent education critics also focused on the inadequate preparation of teachers, and a number of symposia and conferences were held to discuss problems related to this and other aspects of the profession. One of the most influential of these began in 1983 and led to the publication in 1986 of *Tomorrow's Teachers: A Report of the Holmes Group.* From its beginnings with seventeen education deans, this group grew into a collegiate consortium organized around two goals: reforming teacher education and improving the teaching profession. In the words of Judith E. Lanier, chair of the group's executive board, "If for no other reason than the fact that the teachers of teachers should do their graduate work in institutions that have exemplary teacher education programs, a consortium of institutions that educate teacher educators as well as teachers is needed."[44]

In this spirit, the consortium set forth an extensive agenda related to each of its primary objectives. Among other things, The Holmes Group proposed a three-tiered licensing system for teachers. The Instructor's certificate would be a temporary, nonrenewable license whereas the Professional Teacher and Career Professional certificates would be renewable and would carry tenure. Each of these would be granted to teachers on the basis

---

[41] Gardner, *Frames of Mind,* 10.

[42] Curriculum content, expectations or standards, and use of time (time-on-task inside and outside of school, and length of time spent in school annually) were the other three inadequacies. See the National Commission on Excellence in Education, *A Nation at Risk,* 18–23.

[43] Ibid., 30–31.

[44] *Tomorrow's Teachers: A Report of the Holmes Group* (East Lansing, MI: The Holmes Group, Inc., 1986).

of examinations and educational achievements, and granting of the two tenure-bearing credentials would also involve on-the-job performance assessment.[45]

The national commission's influence is quite apparent here, and the influence of both groups is apparent in current practices related to teacher standards. First, many states now require that teacher candidates pass state examinations in order to be certified. Given their pencil-paper nature, however, these tests only measure the prospective teachers' general knowledge in subjects such as mathematics and English, their basic literacy skills (reading comprehension and writing), and their knowledge of content in their specialization or in disciplines in which certification is sought.

In addition, a number of professional organizations have developed special programs to recognize and provide special endorsement for exemplary educators in their disciplines. Although these processes are not free of flaws, they do represent one possible approach to teacher certification and evaluation in which judgments are based upon actual rather than assumed instructional skill.

National Standards in Education

The 1990s have produced, for the first time in American history, a movement toward national education and teacher standards. The Goals 2000: Educate America Act, which seeks in part to establish national competencies in all subjects and for all students across the country, is gaining momentum. This initiative has been especially important for arts education. In the 1960s, those attending the Tanglewood Symposium summarized salient points of their discussions in a statement including the following: "We believe that education must have as major goals the art of living, the building of personal identity, and nurturing creativity. Since the study of music can contribute much to these ends, *we now call for music to be placed in the core of the school curriculum.*" [Emphasis in the original][46] This may finally come to fruition.

The concept of national music and art requirements is supported by professional and educational arts organizations. Since the passage of Goals 2000, the National Consortium of Arts Education Associations, which includes the American Alliance for Theater and Education, the Music Educators National Conference, the National Art Education Association, and the National Dance Association, has formulated standards for student achievement and learning in dance, music, theater, and the visual arts.[47] These standards establish several primary arts objectives for school children in the U.S.: (1) They should learn to communicate at a basic level in dance, music, theater, and the visual arts and at a proficient level in at least one of these disciplines, (2) they should have an "informed acquaintance" with exemplary art works from various cultures and historical periods, (3) they should be able to conduct basic analyses of art works, and (4) they should recog-

[45] Ibid., 10

[46] Robert A. Choate, ed., *Documentary Report of the Tanglewood Symposium* (Washington, DC: Music Educators National Conference, 1968), 139.

[47] See Music Educators National Conference, *National Standards for Arts Education: What every young American should know and be able to do in the Arts* (Reston, VA: Music Educators National Conference, 1994).

nize relationships among various types of arts knowledge and skills and be able to use this knowledge and skills within and across the four arts disciplines.[48]

Standards for dance, music, theater, and the visual arts are presented in grade-level clusters: Grades K–4, grades 5–8, and grades 9–12. Essential interdependent competencies in each of the four disciplines are given for every grade cluster. Because competencies are presented in rather general terms, two kinds of objectives or standards are included to provide additional information. "*Content standards* specify what students should know and be able to do in the arts disciplines. *Achievement standards* specify the understandings and levels of achievement that students are expected to attain in the competencies, for each of the arts, at the completion of grades 4, 8, and 12." [Emphasis in the original][49] Thus, these content and achievement standards assist teachers at all levels of instruction with lesson planning and assessment.

In light of the current consenses and unified efforts of arts organizations, it is likely that significant strides will be made toward securing the arts' position in school curricula and ensuring that all children in the United States at least receive the minimal amount of recommended instruction. Much of the work that needs to be done can begin at the grassroots level with teachers in classrooms, but realization of these goals rests with government officials and education administrators who make decisions about educational programs and expenditures. Ultimately, these people's actions will determine whether the potential inherent in these Goals 2000 art initiatives is actualized.

Multiculturalism and Ethnocentrism

Addressing certain societal problems brings other related concerns to the surface. The notion of equalization, for instance, implies a standard or norm, and by extension, norms imply that something else is abnormal. Since norms are established on the basis of averages and majorities, whether cultural, ethnic, or economic, the very idea of norms has recently been called into question along with educational processes based on them.

Some believe that national mediocrity is a direct result of norms-based education. They reason that the average student's academic achievement has declined as the quality of education has declined. Thus, by basing standards on these lower averages or norms, schools perpetuate mediocrity while failing to meet the needs of students who remain below average or challenge those who are above average. Others suggest that, given the cultural, ethnic, and economic composition of the United States' majority population, norms are unfairly biased for or against various segments of society's young people, particularly when used for developing standardized tests.[50]

Although these debates confirm society's faith in the potential influence of schooling, they also reveal suspicion about motives underlying public education and about the potentially subversive outcomes of it. Concern about what or whose culture is conveyed

---

[48] Ibid., 18–19.

[49] Ibid., 18.

[50] The September–October 1993 issue of *The Long Term View,* a public policy journal issued by the Massachusetts School of Law, titled "Are Standardized Tests Contributing to Social Stratification?" is entirely devoted to these issues.

through formal education, and to what end, continues to exacerbate the uneasy coexistence of ideological and cultural groups. Recently, this issue has become divisive in a country that, at least in theory, applauds and celebrates diversity. Philosophical disagreements about prioritizing the individual versus the group focus today on the relative importance of various ethnic or cultural minorities and the majority.

The current trend is a rather unexpected outcome of civil rights movements of the 1950s and 1960s, which promoted equality and unity and ultimately sought advancement for all minorities. *Multiculturalism* gradually has become an educational concern as a result of the ethnic awareness and sensitivity generated by these movements. Instructional materials dating from the 1960s and 1970s reflect an awareness of cultural diversity and inclusiveness to an extent unprecedented in American schooling. Similarly, teacher education programs began requiring preservice teachers to take courses designed to increase their understanding of ethnic groups and cultures different from their own and to heighten their sensitivity to ethnic differences that had previously been unacknowledged, at least in a positive manner.

Over time, however, ethnic pride engendered or rekindled by general multicultural concerns has led to what some view as being American disunity, educational fragmentation, and a lack of educational focus. Cultural groups have demanded that educational institutions develop and offer courses or curricula specifically related to their heritage and their ethnic group's ideology. Conservative Americans and a number of liberals have begun to speak openly and critically about the divisiveness they generate and the damage they do to earlier civil rights gains.

At the same time, this pride has generated a return to the idea of separate or segregated schooling, which is catching on more and more. Whereas civil rights movements of the 1950s and 1960s were motivated by minority rebellion against segregation, some groups now appear to be in favor of separatist practices. In a number of U.S. cities, various ethnic groups have instituted ethnocentric schools designed to promote a particular cultural frame of reference and point of view. Added to these are other groups—advocates of sex education, education about alternate lifestyles, and prayer in schools; political parties, religious and atheistic organizations; prolife advocates; and the like—who are making their presence felt in American education to a greater extent than in the past.

Multiculturalism in Music Education

Traditionally, school music in U.S. institutions concentrated on Western and European musical cultures. A small number of music educators displayed interest in nonwestern music during the middle years of the progressive period, however, and Karl W. Gherkens's 1924 recommendation that every child receive music instruction awakened other teachers' interest in world music. "At that time, music educators began to make isolated attempts to feature a variety of the world's musics in school programs."[51]

International music education conferences held by MSNC in 1929 and 1931 fueled

---

[51] William M. Anderson and Patricia Shehan Campbell, eds. *Multicultural Perspectives in Music Education* (Reston, VA: Music Educators National Conference, 1989), viii.

this interest, and music education texts including nonwestern music along with pictures depicting life in other cultures also promoted multicultural music teaching and learning. During the 1940s, the United Nations Educational, Scientific, and Cultural Organization's (UNESCO) concern about arts education led to the establishment of the International Music Council, and the combined efforts of these two organizations and others led to the founding of the International Society for Music Education (ISME) in 1953.[52]

From the mid–1950s through the late–1960s, civil rights advocates and student activists emphasized the need for cultural and ethnic awareness. Soon, colleges and universities began offering courses in ethnomusicology,[53] and the 1972 enactment of Public Law 92–318, Title IX sanctioned multicultural education by acknowledging that schooling should provide opportunities for American youth to learn about other cultures. This legislation provided the impetus for multicultural mandates at the state level.[54]

A primary objective of multicultural music education is to provide musical experiences that "encourage and develop [students'] understanding and sensitivity to people from a broad spectrum of ethnic backgrounds."[55] This requires that teachers distinguish between (1) using music of other cultures in lessons focusing on concepts and practices associated with western music, and (2) teaching music of other cultures in ways that offer insight into the musical practices and general characteristics of those cultures. Although both approaches may familiarize students with a variety of world musics, only the second approach constitutes multicultural music education. Hence, when planning multicultural experiences for their classes, music educators must consider two important issues—authenticity, and the importance of musical differences.

Many factors affect *authenticity* (how closely a performance of music from another culture matches performances of the same music by members of that culture). One of these factors—taking music from its original culture and putting it into another—is unavoidable, but teachers must be aware that music automatically loses some of its essential qualities when it is transferred from one culture to another.[56] Moreover, each additional change to that music (i.e., translating text, using different performance media, using different tuning systems) lessens the music's authenticity. Some simplification or adaptation may be necessary, but there is usually a point at which the music loses the essence so that it no longer represents the tradition under study.[57] There are several reasons for this phenomenon, but one the most important of these is that teachers frequently do not take care to preserve im-

---

[52] Joyce Jordan, "Multicultural Music Education in a Pluralistic Society," in *Handbook of Research on Music Teaching and Learning,* ed. Richard Colwell (New York: Schirmer Books, 1992), 735; Jack Cobb, "International Society for Music Education Forty Years Old," *International Journal of Music Education* 22 (1993), 4–8.

[53] *Ethnomusicology* is "the comparative study of the world's musical cultures, from a relativistic perspective." Most of the research done by ethnomusicologists focuses on music in tribal societies and villages and "the cultivated music of professional musicians in geographically restricted areas." Bruno Nettl, "Ethnomusicology and the Teaching of World Music," *International Journal of Music Education* 20 (1992), 3.

[54] Jordan, "Multicultural Music Education in a Pluralistic Society," 735–736.

[55] Anderson and Campbell, *Multicultural Perspectives in Music Education,* 1.

[56] Anthony J. Palmer, "World Musics in Music Education: The Matter of Authenticity," *International Journal of Music Education* 19 (1992), 33.

[57] Palmer, "World Musics in Music Education," 32.

portant differences between western music and the music of other ethnic and cultural groups.

American music educators tend to teach music of other cultures from a western musical perspective, applying understandings derived from this music to various world musics. This practice is understandable, but it may also be counterproductive. First, western music and the music of other ethnic groups involve many of the same elements but define them differently. Consider, for example, that although the music of other cultures involves pitch, these cultures may not refer to these pitches as "low" or "high". Also, western cultures usually consider the first beat of a unit or measure as the strongest whereas other cultures frequently accent another beat in the metric unit. In some cultures, the lowest pitch in a mode does not function the same way as western music's tonic or key-note, and other ethnic groups have very different ways of classifying musical instruments.[58] All of these differences are important because they reflect the essential nature of various cultural groups. Ultimately, music and culture are inseparable. People who understand how another culture "knows" music will also understands how that culture "knows" most things. In this way, understanding the music of other ethnic groups leads to multicultural understanding on a profound level.

Clearly, teaching world music as a means to cultural understanding involves more than using music of other cultures in a music lesson. For reasons discussed above, teachers must spend considerable time learning about other cultures, their music, and their musical practices in order to present these to students effectively. A large number of resources are available, most of which include textual information about various cultures, their histories and traditions, and their music. These resources may also include notated selections of music from different cultures along with translations and pronunciation guides. Other resources include audio or video recordings featuring various ethnic groups performing music of their culture.[59] Research studies conducted by ethnomusicologists also provide materials and documents that teachers interested in learning about various world musics can use for personal study or as part of classroom presentations.[60]

Just as many general music educators at all educational levels are including music of various cultures in general music instruction, a good number of ensemble directors at various educational levels are including music of nonwestern and other cultures in their repertoire selections. Similarly, many ensemble directors, particularly those at the secondary and college levels have expanded their institutions' ensemble offerings to include groups that focus or specialize in jazz, gospel, or some other type of non-classical music. All of these curricular changes constitute efforts to broaden the range of musical experiences students obtain in public school music programs and to increase cross-cultural understanding.

---

[58] Robert Walker, "Music and Multiculturalism," *International Journal of Music Education* 8 (1986), 43.

[59] *Multicultural Perspectives in Music Education* by Anderson and Campbell, for instance, is available as part of a package including video tapes featuring music and information about Asian Americans, African Americans, Hispanic Americans, and American Indians. A two-cassette sampler, *Music Resources for Multicultural Perspectives* is available separately for use as a classroom resource.

[60] William M. Anderson, *Teaching Music with a Multicultural Approach* (Reston, VA: Music Educators National Conference, 1991), vii.

Interdisciplinary Education and Thematic Teaching

As is the case with many current trends in education, interdisciplinary education was prac-ticed centuries ago when it was believed that knowledge about the separate disciplines pro-vided insight into the world and existence and ultimately led to wisdom. Although aca-demic and artistic disciplines have become more and more distinct and specialized over time, current core curriculum requirements, particularly at the high school and college lev-els, stem in part from very similar objectives: (1) to provide a well-rounded education for students, regardless of their specialization; (2) to encourage the transfer of more-or-less generic skills from one discipline to another; and (3) to diminish the fragmentation of knowledge fostered by specialization.

Since the1980s, *interdisciplinarity* has again gained widespread support and has be-come a popular instructional approach among educators at all levels of education. As used in today's schools, it is defined as "a knowledge view and curriculum approach that con-sciously applies methodology and language from more than one discipline to examine a central theme, issue, problem, topic, or experience."[61] Its primary objectives are funda-mentally the same as they have always been, however. Each discipline retains its unique qualities and students study it because of its own worth, but skills and concepts from other disciplines are used to illustrate, clarify, or elaborate on some facet of it.

During a seventh grade general music lesson, for instance, a music teacher who is presenting the concept of phrase length may ask the students to draw parallels between the lengths of phrases heard in a recorded selection and the lengths of lines used in a water-color painting. The teacher may then lead the students in singing a well-known song while they draw its phrases on a sheet of paper, reminding them to start a new line for each new phrase. Next, the teacher and students may read through one or two short poems and com-pare each poet's phrases with the recorded selection and painting. One of the students points out that the "lines" in all of these are the same, and since all of these materials hap-pen to date from the same era, the teacher spends a few minutes explaining relationships between phrase lengths and other aspects of life during that period. By the end of the class period, the teacher has used literature, visual arts, movement, and history to reinforce a musical idea.

Schools throughout the country currently use interdisciplinary instruction in a vari-ety of formats, from study units developed by a single teacher to units or courses that are team-taught by several teachers. When used effectively, this approach to teaching and learning facilitates the use of higher-order thinking and analytical skills, encourages the transfer of learning, and aids retention of information.

Thematic teaching, a simplified form of interdisciplinary instruction, is used at the grade-school level. In thematic lessons or units, teachers and students explore the selected topic or issue simultaneously through various academic and artistic subjects so that students acquire a holistic understanding of it. Rather than helping these young students formulate relationships among disciplines or transfer knowledge and skills from one dis-

---

[61] Heidi Hayes Jacobs, ed., *Interdisciplinary Curriculum: Design and Implementation* (Alexandria, VA: Association for Supervision and Curriculum Development, 1989), 8. Also see Julie Thompson Klein, *Interdisci-plinary: History, Theory, and Practice* (Detroit: Wayne State University Press, 1990).

cipline to another, thematic lessons help the children understand topics or issues or acquire the desired skills. Some elementary schools have theme days in which all of the students, teachers, administrators, and parents participate whereas in other schools, curriculum organization for the entire year focuses on various themes or topics.

Problems stemming from these educational approaches include scheduling, attaining specific grade-level or subject-area objectives, providing more than a superficial coverage of important discipline-specific knowledge, and a tendency to draw spurious, inaccurate, or forced parallels between various subjects. If carefully and thoughtfully planned, however, interdisciplinary education can be worthwhile for students and teachers alike.

REFERENCES AND RECOMMENDED SOURCES

ADLER, MORTIMER J. *The Paideia Proposal: An Educational Syllabus.* New York: Macmillan Publishing, 1984.

————. *Paideia Problems and Possibilities.* New York: Macmillan Publishing Co., 1983.

————. *The Paideia Proposal: An Educational Manifesto.* New York: Macmillan Publishing, 1982.

AIEX, NOLA KORTNER. "Home Schooling and Socialization of Children." *ERIC Digest* (1994). ERIC, ED 372 460

AIEX, PATRICK K. *Home Schooling, Socialization, and Creativity in Children.* (April 1994). ERIC, ED 367 040.

ANDERSON, WILLIAM M. *Teaching Music with a Multicultural Approach.* Reston, VA: Music Educators National Conference, 1991.

————, and PATRICIAN SHEHAN CAMPBELL, eds. *Multicultural Perspectives in Music Education.* Reston, VA: Music Educators National Conference, 1989.

————, eds. *Music Resources for Multicultural Perspectives.* Cassette recording. Reston, VA: Music Educators National Conference, 1989.

ARMSTRONG, THOMAS. *Multiple Intelligences in the Classroom.* Alexandria, VA: Association for Supervision and Curriculum Development, 1994.

BAST, JOSEPH L., AND HERBERT J. WALBERG. "Free Market Choice: Can Education Be Privatized?" In *Radical Education Reforms,* Chester E. Finn and Herbert J. Walberg, eds. Berkeley, CA: McCutchan Publishing Corporation, 1994.

BENNETT, WILLIAM J. *Our Country and Our Children.* New York: Simon and Schuster, 1988.

CAIRNS, JOHN A. "Charter Schools in Minnesota." In *Radical Education Reforms,* Chester E. Finn and Herbert J. Walberg, eds. Berkeley, CA: McCutchan Publishing Corporation, 1994.

CALVERY, ROBERT, DAVID BELL, AND CARL VAUPEL. *The Difference in Achievement between Home Schooled and Public Schooled Students in Grades Four, Seven, and Ten in Arkansas.* Paper presented at the annual meeting of the Mid-South Educational Research Association, Knoxville, TN, 11–13 November 1992. ERIC, ED 354 248.

CHOATE, ROBERT A., ED. *Documentary Report of the Tanglewood Symposium.* Washington, DC: Music Educators National Conference, 1968.

COBB, JACK. "International Society for Music Education Forty Years Old." *International Journal of Music Education* 22 (1993): 4–8.

COLFAX, DAVID, AND MICKI COLFAX. *Homeschooling for Excellence.* New York: Warner Books, 1988.

CREMIN, LAWRENCE A. *Popular Education and Its Discontents.* New York: Harper and Row, 1990.

DRUCKER, PETER. *The Age of Discontinuity: Guidelines to Our Changing Society.* New York: Harper and Row, 1968; reprint, New Brunswick, NJ: Transaction Publishers, 1992.

FINN CHESTER E., AND HERBERT J. WALBERG, EDS. *Radical Education Reforms.* Berkeley, CA: McCutchan Publishing Corporation, 1994.

GARDNER, HOWARD. *Frames of Mind: The Theory of Multiple Intelligences.* New York: Basic Books, 1983; paperback ed. with introduction by Howard Gardner. New York: Basic Books, 1985.

———. *Multiple Intelligences: The Theory in Practice.* New York: Basic Books, 1993.

HARRINGTON-LUEKER, DONNA. "Charter 'Profit'." *American School Board Journal* (September 1994): 27–28.

———. "Charter Schools," *American School Board Journal* 181 (September 1994): 22–26.

Health, Education, and Human Services Division. *Charter Schools: New Models for Public Schools Provides Opportunities and Challenges.* Report to Congressional Registers. Gaitherburg, MD: U.S. General Accounting Office, 1995. ERIC, ED 378 702.

HECHINGER, NANCY. "Technology in the Edison Schools." In *Radical Education Reforms,* Chester E. Finn and Herbert J. Walberg, eds. Berkeley, CA: McCutchan Publishing Corporation, 1994.

HEISE, MICHAEL. "New School Choice Plans." In *Radical Education Reforms,* Chester E. Finn and Herbert J. Walberg, eds. Berkeley, CA: McCutchan Publishing Corporation, 1994.

HEUSTON, DUSTIN H. "Technology in School Improvement." In *Radical Education Reforms,* Chester E. Finn and Herbert J. Walberg, eds. Berkeley, CA: McCutchan Publishing Corporation, 1994.

HILL, PAUL T. "Reinventing Urban Public Education." *Phi Delta Kappan* 75 (January 1994): 396–401.

JACOBS, HEIDI HAYES, ED. *Interdisciplinary Curriculum: Design and Implementation.* Alexandria, VA: Association for Supervision and Curriculum Development, 1989.

JORDAN, JOYCE. "Multicultural Music Education in a Pluralistic Society." In *Handbook of Research on Music Teaching and Learning,* ed. Richard Colwell, 735–748. New York: Schirmer Books, 1992.

KLEIN, JULIE THOMPSON. *Interdisciplinarity: History, Theory, and Practice.* Detroit: Wayne State University Press, 1990.

LIEBERMAN, MYRON. *Privatization and Educational Choice.* New York: St. Martin's Press, 1989.

LINES, PATRICIA M. *Estimating the Home Schooled Population.* Working paper prepared for the Office of Education Research and Improvement. Washington, DC: U.S. Department of Education, 1991. ERIC, ED 337 903.

————. "Home Schooling." *ERIC Digest* (April 1995). ERIC, ED 381 849.

Massachusetts School of Law at Andover. *The Long View* 1 (September-October 1993).

MAYBERRY, MARALEE. *Conflict and Social Determinisim: The Reprivatization of Education.* Paper presented at the annual meeting of the American Educational Research Association, Chicago, IL, 3–7 April 1991. ERIC, ED 330 107.

MEIER, DEBORAH. "Central Park East: An Alternative Story." *Skole* 4–8 (1988—1992): 122–134, ed. Mary M. Leue. ERIC, ED 360 126.

MOORE, BRAIN. "Future Technology: Working for Education." *Music Educators Journal* (November 1992): 30–32, 67.

Music Educators National Conference. *National Standards for Arts Education: What every young American should know and be able to do in the Arts.* Reston, VA: Music Educators National Conference, 1994.

NATALE, JO ANNA. "The Attraction of the Arts." *Music Educators Journal* (December 1992): 46–48.

National Commission on Excellence in Education. *A Nation at Risk: The Imperative for Educational Reform.* A Report to the Nation and the U.S. Secretary of Education. Washington, DC: Government Printing Office, 1983.

A National Study of Home Education. Paeonian Springs, VA: Home School Legal Defense Association, 1990. ERIC, ED 381 725.

NEILL, A. S. *Summerhill: A Radical Approach to Child Rearing.* With a foreword by Erich Fromm. New York: Pocket Books, 1960.

NETTL, BRUNO. "Ethnomusicology and the Teaching of World Music." *International Journal of Music Education* 20 (1992): 3–7.

NEWHILL, SHARON L. *The Paseo Fine and Performing Arts Magnet High School, 1989–1990, 1990–1991, 1991–1992: Summative Evaluation.* Kansas City, MO: Kansas City School District, 1992. ERIC, ED 380 387.

NYQUIST, EWALD B., AND GENE R. HAWES, EDS. *Open Education: A Sourcebook for Parents and Teachers.* New York: Bantam Books, 1972.

PALMER, ANTHONY J. "World Musics in Music Education: The Matter of Authenticity." *International Journal of Music Education* 19 (1992): 32–40.

PETERS, G. DAVID. "Music Software and Emerging Technology." *Music Educators Journal* (November 1992): 22–25, 63.

RAVITCH, DIANE. *The Troubled Crusade: American Education, 1945–1980.* New York: Basic Books, 1983.

RIST, MARILEE C. "Here Comes 'McSchool'." *American School Board Journal* 178 (September 1991): 30–31.

SAKS, JUDITH BRODY. "Scrutinizing Edison." *American School Board Journal* 182 (February 1995): 20–25.

VON SEGGERN, MARILYN.   "Magnet Music Programs: A Look at the Issues." *Music Educators Journal* (March 1990): 50–53.

SIZER, THEODORE R.   *Horace's School: Redesigning the American High School.* Boston, MA: Houghton Mifflin, 1992.

———.   "Rebuilding: First Steps." *Skole* 4–8 (1988–1992): 135–148, ed. Mary M. Leue. ERIC, ED 360 126.

SPRING, JOEL.   *The American School: 1642–1990.* 2d ed. New York: Longman, 1990.

Tomorrow's Teachers: A Report of The Holmes Group. East Lansing, MI: The Holmes Group, 1986.

TOPAZ, MURIEL.   "Something New Is in the Air: Arts Magnet High Schools." *Dance Magazine* (April 1995): 100–103.

WAGNER, TONY.   *How Schools Change: Lessons from Three Communities.* Boston, MA: Beacon Press, 1994.

WALKER, ROBERT.   "Music and Multiculturalism." *International Journal of Music Education* 8 (1986): 43–50.

WHITEHEAD, JOHN W., AND ALEXIS IRENE CROW.   *Home Education: Rights and Reasons.* Wheaton, IL: Crossway Books, 1993.

WILLIAMS, DAVID BRIAN, AND PETER RICHARD WEBSTER.   *Experiencing Music Technology: Software, Data, and Hardware.* New York: Schirmer Books, 1996.

WOOD, GEORGE.   *Schools that Work: America's Most Innovative Public Education Programs.* New York: NAL, 1992.

7

Where Does Music Education Go from Here?

It seems appropriate to begin the final chapter of this text by reiterating its underlying premises: (1) The status of music education in any society reflects general philosophical viewpoints about the nature of music, its purpose, and its value; and (2) music education history reveals recurring themes or cycles on which shrewd guesses about the discipline's future can be based.

This presentation has explored U.S. music education, its history and European heritage, its institution in school programs, its prosperous times and its problematic ones. During the presentation, perhaps even in the opening chapter, it undoubtedly became apparent that educational developments, whether in music or in general education, tend to go in cycles. Good times are usually followed by difficult ones. Financially trying periods seem to be followed by more prosperous times. Declines in educational achievement are followed by cries for educational reform.

History becomes progress when thinking is made more effective by learning from the experiences of past generations and using those experiences to enlighten one's own. New generations should not have to reinvent the wheel. "Progress by acquisition," as opposed to evolution by inheritance, is measured in generations. Human beings develop their potential, in part, by building on knowledge acquired from the past.[1]

History begins when the passage of time is viewed as "a series of specific events in which men are consciously involved and which they can consciously influence [rather than accepting things as they are]."[2] If this is indeed the case, then everyone can contribute in some way to the history of music in U.S. schools.

In this spirit, the authors pose a final question: What does the future hold for music education? For general education? Five, ten, fifteen years from now, what can one expect

---

[1] Edward Hallett Carr, *What Is History?* (New York: Vintage Books, 1961), 150.
[2] Ibid., 178.

the situation to be in American education? Use the knowledge and understanding acquired from this text to speculate about the future of music instruction in public schools. While there is no single correct response, hypotheses should be based on lessons that history and current practice teach. Think about each of the following while formulating a response:

First, what will society be like by the middle of the twenty-first century? Descriptions should include such issues as:

1. how societal goals for education will be different from those discussed in this text
2. how society will perceive the music education profession and discipline
3. how education will be structured (e.g., the length of the school day, its subject matter and curricular offerings)
4. the status of compulsory schooling

Next, consider the philosophy of music education, past and present. Speculate about what it will be by the middle of the twenty-first century. Include such things as

1. what music meant in the past, what it means now, and what it may mean in the future
2. what the philosophy of music should be in the twenty-first century

Now consider past and present ways of teaching music and speculate about changes that may be required in the future, if any. Include the following:

1. what learning is, how it is acquired, and how these will be different for the next generation
2. domains of learning and learning styles
3. how human development affects learning and thinking
4. the "spiral curriculum" concept
5. various types of instructional materials, particularly computers and other electronic devices

Given your responses to the preceding questions and information in this text, discuss ways in which teacher preparation may be different by the middle of the twenty-first century. Consider the following:

1. preservice and in-service needs
2. continuing education requirements for teachers

Finally, discuss at least two problems that the music education profession may have to address through professional seminars, conferences, or projects. This discussion should consider:

1. the rationale for the conference
2. possible organizational formats for the conference
3. why the conference will be necessary, who will attend, and what its goals would be

Index